The Book of Honor: Chosen to Teach and to Tell

Veronica Y. Njeri-Imani

Xulon PRESS

The Book of Honor: Chosen to Teach and to Tell
by Veronica Y. Njeri-Imani

Printed in the United States of America

ISBN 9781624199585

www.xulonpress.com

Table of Contents

Acknowledgements

*H*eavenly Father, I thank You first for giving me
life abundantly through Jesus Christ my Savior.
I love my parents, grandparents, my siblings and their
peeps, too. Miss Thompson, I can only remember your
kind, Christian heart in Sunday School.

To Pam McLaughlin, my editor, I appreciate everything you saw in this project, especially for the sake of
women in the struggle.

To my pastor and those in the local churches where
I was accepted into the fold, may God continue to
bless your work in a world that needs the Lord God
more than ever.

To the sisters of the Franciscan Order in New York
City, you loved me and my best friend unconditionally
after college ended. Hallelujah!

To the restaurant owners in the USA who believed
in me and gave me employment, you have the best taste!

To the brave dorm and apartment company man-
agement, you showed me to value space and time with
my resources.

Aarons, the teachers, the Rachels, my best Black
sister-friends, my favorite school principals, and USA
government leaders—you were chosen for my generation's success.

My literary agent Dr. Larry Keefauver expected me to appreciate my health care providers, too, so this book is possible because my students gave me hope and a renewed commitment to being my beautiful, most healthy self. Grace unto you all!

Learning to Drive by 35

*T*earned my Arizona driver's license a short time
before my 35th birthday. It was like a miracle
given the struggle I had since adolescence to obtain
one. When I was fifteen, my mother came into my
bedroom early one morning and announced that I was
going to Raines, the local high school near our neighborhood, to learn how to drive. My Dad took me to
the Jacksonville Florida Department of Motor Vehicles
to get my driver's permit, and I rode drove down the
street successfully with him. My mother only took me
out driving in our neighborhood once, even though
I explained to her that the instructor encouraged us
to practice outside of class since there were so many
students there.

She did not understand. To this day, my parents
do not realize the effect their arguments had on me.
My father took me driving once for about an hour,
landing in the parking lot of my mother's job at a
clinic in her car. I overheard their loud voices as she
told my father that I was a teenager and would not be
going on her insurance. My heart sank. What was the
point of enrolling me in the course and my going each
weekday and earning a "C" if I would not be covered
and allowed to drive a car? My father had used cars that

he believed only he could maneuver, so I was not going to be permitted to use his vehicle, either.

My class standing at the Douglas Anderson School of the Arts, formerly an all-African American high school under segregation, would have been higher without that average grade. I dropped the course as God worked things out in my favor. I was the only person of color in the top ten in my graduating class in 1990. My mother stood with me crying as we hugged each other in celebration as they called me up to accept each award.

In college I rode a bicycle, took public transit, and walked to go where I needed to be. I also took rides with people whom I trusted and learned how to hire a taxicab. In my late twenties, people from church gave me a few lessons in their vehicles before I paid to go to driving school. The kind, white-haired European American woman who was my instructor did not tell me when we were going out onto the street on purpose so I would not be nervous. She helped me to "go forward" out onto the open road just as the Lord God provided for Moses and the children of Israel to do after they left Egypt: "And the Lord said unto Moses, 'Wherefore criest thou unto me? Speak unto the children of Israel, that they go forward'." (Exodus 14:15). In the end, a health care agency found a grant for me to be taught and tested as a driver before the instructor issued me a license.

It is crucial that American women have reliable, safe ways to go places as we do things in this part of God's kingdom. The enemy of our souls cannot be allowed to use technology against us where we need it the most. Being available to God in the church and in our families makes us truly Christ's women. A great example of this was my maternal grandmother whom I affectionately call, "Grandmama." Maybe there was something about her boarding a bus and riding down to Miami to show her first grandchild to her young sister that stuck with me. Family is so very important, and this memoir is about how God chose me to be a part of His Family.

God told the Prophet Jeremiah that he had a special calling to serve Him:

"Before I formed you in the womb I knew you" (Jeremiah 1:5 NKJV).

The Lord has declared to me through Peter, one of His faithful disciples,

"But you are chosen generation, a royal priesthood, a holy nation, His own special people, that you may proclaim the praises of Him who called you out of darkness into His marvelous light" (I Peter 2:9 NKJV).

To me, being chosen by God for His purposes is the highest honor. The Lord God placed within me the gifts of teaching and writing: "There are diversities of gifts, but the same Spirit. There are differences of ministries, but the same Lord. And there are diversities of activities, but it is the same God who works all in all. But the manifestation of the Spirit is given to each one for the profit of all: for to one is given the word of wisdom through the Spirit, to another the word of knowledge through the same Spirit" (I Corinthians 12:4-8).

Throughout my life, God has placed me in the tutelage of teachers from around the world who imparted to me important lessons. Being a young, African American woman teacher at the university level empowered me to bless students who needed the information and understanding I had in order to move forward in their majors, and in preparation for their careers. This testimony that I offer to Him I share with you because of the time we live in, and the time that is approaching when we will face the Lord God the Judge to give an account of how we used the lives He gave to us as the Creator to live for Him. My anointing, mistakes, suffering, tests, trials, tribulation, and triumphs make me who I am—the daughter of God.

The King and Kindergarten

When I was a little girl, school seemed to be the safest place. Adults did not call each other ugly names in front of children. They never beat one another up. I attended church school on the Sabbath, learning about the characters and stories of *The Holy Bible*. From kindergarten to my senior year of high school, classrooms where I grew academically and artistically mostly felt like play.

I attended kindergarten along with my two younger brothers in the home of a well-to-do husband and wife who knew my parents from church. The couple had several handsome sons who are very accomplished today. Located in a separate part of the large, split level house were the classroom, lunchroom, nap room, and bathroom. The huge, grassy backyard included a large playground set where we spent recess. The teacher, a petite, light-skinned woman, picked us up in the morning in her station wagon and dropped us off at home in the late afternoon. I really believe that she loved children and followed the teaching that the Lord Jesus gave to His disciples when He told them, "Let the little children come to Me, and do not forbid them; for of such is the kingdom of God" (Mark 10:14).

The curriculum included the alphabet, math, and Bible songs. "Jesus Loves Me," "Jesus Loves the Little Children," and "Father Abraham" are Christian songs that I learned as a little girl and still adore today. Kindergarten reinforced the biblical learning I received at home and in church about Jesus Christ the King of kings. It also prepared me for success in elementary school and enrollment in the Duval County of Florida's gifted program.

Young, Gifted, Female, and Brown-Skinned

I am young, gifted, female, and brown-skinned.
In the sixth grade, I was enrolled in Duval County's gifted program. A few times during the week, I rode a school bus with two white boys to George Washington Carver Elementary School. One of my classmates had dark hair; the other one had blond hair. They joked with each other like brothers and treated me like a girl. As I grew closer to my teenaged years, I began to notice how people treated me and other African American young people differently, as though we were threats to white hegemony.

W.E.B. Du Bois describes in the classic collection of essays *The Souls of Black Folk* (1903) as the "color line"—"The problem of the twentieth century is the problem of the color line,—the relation of the darker to the lighter races of men in Asia and Africa, in America and the islands of the sea."[1]

The young, European American woman who taught our class made a lasting impact upon me. One day, she assigned an exercise wherein we were required to decide who would live and who would die after a scientist made a major mistake. Did the scientist deserve to live since his wife was pregnant? What would become of the man suffering from alcoholism? I was never sure why we were given this assignment. Perhaps it was because our teacher did not conclude the exercise by commenting on consequences. Who in society has the power to make life and death decisions and why? Since prayer had been banned from schools by this time, we were not encouraged to talk about God in this lesson.

For another assignment, we were to write about Florida history. Early one morning, students from across the county boarded charter buses to ride to the capital in Tallahassee. The schedule included visiting Florida State University (FSU) but not Florida A&M University (FAMU), a historically Black university (HBCU). My mother drove me and my grandmother there and noted how isolated I seemed to be from the white children. The only other students of color were an African American boy and Filipino American boy. To protect me, my family separated from the group, and we did our own tour of Tallahassee.

The last recollection I have of being in the gifted program involved the one day that our teacher arranged for us to play kickball with a traditional class of students. All of them were African American boys. My white male classmates felt very intimidated by them. Their opponents were tough and the black boys won the game. My sour-faced classmates and I returned to the classroom, soiled and tired.

I remembered how in the third grade, a European American woman came in to teach remedial reading to the "slow" students several times during the month. Our teacher, a stern, African American woman with a red Afro, paddled me in my hand because I asked the reading teacher to be considerate. Some of the rest of us in the class could not concentrate on our lessons due to the noise.

I respected my teacher for showing us a film about African American abolitionist Harriet Tubman, Conductor on the "Underground Railroad" for social studies.[2] Although I felt she had been a little harsh towards me, I remember how one day she saw me walking and said, "Hold your head up like a model." It was not until I started reading books in my Dad's library in senior high school that I realized how widespread the systematic tracking of African American students into special education classes actually is in the United States.

Later at Spelman College, an African American woman mathematician who had graduated from the Massachusetts Institute of Technology (MIT) delivered a lecture on this same topic, and challenged us as student leaders to recognize the giftedness of black children. I am grateful to God that I am one of the blessed ones who escaped being marked as "disadvantaged" and "at-risk" as a black girl-child, and that someone—family, teachers, community leaders—saw the brilliance in me and helped me to stand apart as a young leader.

Twelve

$\mathcal{M}$y personal relationship with Jesus Christ began when I was twelve. According to my pastel baby book, I started to pray at the age of two. Dad, as the priest of our household started attending the historically African American Bethel Baptist Institutional Church. My Sunday School teacher then was truly a woman who loved children. She looked so elegant in her Coco Chanel-style suits, hats, and nice jewelry. She represented the kind of woman I wanted to become. For the first time after years of being taught the Bible at home, appearing in Easter Sunday pageants, and attending different churches, I understood what salvation through Jesus Christ as written in John 3:16 was all about: "For God so loved the world that He gave His only begotten Son, that whoever believes in Him should not perish but have everlasting life."

The Sunday after my youngest brother dedicated himself to the Lord, I walked down the aisle and gave my life to Christ. Even as a child and especially as one living in a space where domestic violence was present, I knew I would be helpless without Him. Tears streamed down my cheeks as I made my way down to the altar. On the day that my brother and I were baptized, I wore my favorite pink dress and was baptized by immersion.

My Dad was so proud that he took pictures of us following the Lord's example. My other younger brother was baptized a short time later.

My mother has kept all of our membership certificates in a special place. On Sunday mornings she gave me silver coins and taught me about the tithe. The Holy Bible is clear about raising godly children: "Train up a child in the way he should go, and when he is old he will not depart from it" (Proverbs 22:6). I am grateful to the Lord God for placing me in a home where each of us were given a *Holy Bible,* and where worshipping God on the Sabbath were important. Although I am saddened by the dysfunction that existed in my family, my parents gave me the most important tool for knowing how to live a life that pleases God.

The Gifts God Gave to Me

Teaching and writing are the gifts God gave to me. Excellent oral communication skills have helped me in relationships with the people I love and those I have worked with artistically, in business, and as an educator. Superb writing skills led me to a career as a college composition teacher and a writer. My parents taught me to pray and to read *The Holy Bible* at an early age, and I learned to value the spoken and the written word. I started out in private school which I attended from kindergarten through the second grade. The value-based curriculum and small class size provided the perfect environment for my mind to soak up ideas like a sponge.

When I arrived at the public school in the third grade, I noticed that the textbook we used for language arts was the same one that the teacher taught out of in the second grade at the private school, aptly named Kiddie Kollege on Jacksonville's Northside. Sadly, I found that several of my schoolmates wasted their words by cursing and playing dumb to be popular with their do-nothing peers who preferred to be clowns rather than good students. A few of the students had serious behavioral problems. One afternoon, two African American boys, one short and one tall, terrorized me by grabbing and pulling on my body including my private parts. I tried to fight them off as the African American female dean stood watching and did nothing.

I decided not to be like kids who hated school, but strove to be an "A" student. In the third grade, I won the title of "Most Courteous Student" which gave me the honor of addressing the entire student body on the intercom. This was the same intercom that played *The Lord's Prayer* every morning.

In the fifth grade, I wrote a book about seashells after a field trip to a marine biology park on the beach. Small, pastel coquinas floated across the pages near cockle and scallop shells. I was blessed to find a scallop shell to take home.

That same year, I started writing and illustrating a book about a poor, dark Puerto Rican little girl, a wishing well, and a wicked witch. I never got it back from my teacher, but to this day I remember how my parents' gift of Hans Christian Andersen stories inspired me to write tales of my own.[3] The seed of literacy was planted by my parents, especially my mother, who took my brothers and me to the public library to check out books at a young age.

My mother fought the bureaucracy to have me enrolled in Stanton College Preparatory School for the seventh grade. Both of my parents are alumni of the New Stanton High School. Sadly, students were not told of Stanton's history as an important school for African Americans since the 19th century.

"Immediately after Emancipation, a group of colored people in the City of Jacksonville organized themselves into the Education Society, and on February 8, 1868, purchased the property on which the Stanton School Building now stands from Ossian B. Hart and his wife ....[In] December of that year...the first school was built and incorporated through the aid of the Freedman's Bureau. The school was a wooden structure and was named in honor of General Edwin McMasters Stanton, President Abraham Lincoln's Secretary of War....It was the first school of education for black children in Jacksonville... and was the first school for black children in the State of Florida." Stanton offered "vocational" education and "at night, it became a center for the Adult and Veterans Education Program. During the 1980-1981 school year the focus of New Stanton High School changed again. It became one of the magnet schools instituted by the Duval County School Board to serve gifted student throughout the county. Hence, the name was changed to Stanton College Preparatory School."[4]

The academic rigor of Stanton prepared me for high school graduation and for college. To this day, it remains a National Model School.

By the ninth grade, I understood that my writing could entertain others. During a lesson on personification, my English teacher at Stanton conveyed how to make something seem alive using the right words. I imagined what it would be like to be a can of soda and wrote an imagery speech that I believed it would have. Little did I know that at Open House, my teacher would read my essay aloud as an example of good writing. People including my grandmother laughed at the funny parts. That evening, I experienced the importance of knowing your audience.

Teenage Years,
Teenage Lessons

*A*cademics comprised much of my teenage life. To me, there was nothing more important than earning good grades in order to have a bright future. I had two younger brothers who were watching everything I did, so there was no room for messing up. Not one time did I ever bring a sex-crazed boyfriend, alcohol, or drugs into my father's house. Instead, I maintained the youth newsletter that I founded at our church, and sang in the choir. The best time of my life up until that point was when I spent time with my peers at church.

At thirteen, I officially became a teenager. It was my second year at Stanton College Preparatory School where we changed classes after each period. Once again as it had been in the seventh grade, my elective was visual art. My teacher liked students and encouraged our creativity. She was a mother, and her daughter attended our school. Our class was talented. I won a blue ribbon prize from the Savannah College of Art and Design for a multimedia portrait I created of a live model. It was an honor to go the reception with my mother and to represent my family and my school. My father's artistry had been passed down to me, his daughter. As *The Holy Bible* promises, "A man's gift makes room for him, and brings him before great men" (Proverbs 18:16). I embraced this heritage and developed artistic skills strong enough for competition.

High School

In high school, I opened up and appeared to be a true extrovert. Focusing on my lessons and doing as my teachers told me to do were my goals. I was still an "A" student and loved learning. After dinner, I talked to my best friends on the telephone about faith, boys, and music.

Typing class provided me with a necessary skill for success as a writer. In the ninth grade, my teacher was a sweet, African American woman. Very pregnant, she walked between the rows of desks as we learned the keys and strokes. One day, she called me to her desk and spoke to me softly about class. For the rest of the course, my typing teacher let me know that she cared about my success and that I was a special student. I had always been fascinated by typewriters, the letters and meaningful sentences they formed. Once, I accidentally dropped the home office typewriter on my foot and injured my toe pretty badly. Too afraid of being punished to tell my parents who would then be forced to pay a hospital bill, I limped for weeks in summer school until God healed my toe. My Dad purchased a large, IBM model that I practiced on to master a higher typing speed.

At my father's house, my brothers and I were taught how black people must be twice as good as whites and to have a strong work ethic. Nothing made my parents' lesson on African American struggle more poignant than the hours we spent as we sat together and watched

Eyes on the Prize, the documentary series on the modern civil rights movement aired on PBS.[5] I felt sickened by the brutality of the Southern white citizens and officials, but energized by the godly courage of my people who employed nonviolence to change America.

Sleeping in on Sundays was not an option. At one point, my parents taught Sunday School at our church. This was when most Christian Americans dressed up for worship service. My mother spent hard-earned money so that the three of us would be presentable in new clothes. Oftentimes, I went with her on those shopping trips at the mall. Although she still worked full-time as a nurse, she cooked nutritious dinners for us and made sure we did our homework. I began to share the responsibility of cooking and shopping for groceries with her.

I was fourteen years old when I first visited the dentist. One of my younger brothers had gone before me. My father had a new job with the city that made it possible for all three of us to go to the dentist on the same day. A kind, Asian American woman dentist and an African American woman dental assistant worked on my teeth although the practice was owned by a prominent African American man dentist. The drilling and sucking noises did not scare me for I was relieved to be having my health care needs met. It is hard being a daughter in a world that favors sons. I have since been told that I have a beautiful smile and good teeth.

Fifteen

At the age of fifteen, I had a grand birthday party. My friends from school came and wished me a happy birthday with their presence and thoughtful cards and gifts. My youngest brother provided the entertainment by dancing for us. My other younger brother made tuna salad that was quite delicious alongside the other party foods that my mother had prepared. My father, who bought Michael Jackson's *Thriller* album for us, gave me Janet Jackson's debut album *Control*. We ate cake and ice cream, and I did a few makeovers for my friends. This birthday was very special for me.

I was inspired by my high school teachers who encouraged and even praised my writing. In the tenth grade, my English teacher who shared the story of her family's migration to America from Europe, read passages from the essay I wrote about the coming-of-age novel *A Separate Peace* by John Knowles (1959) to the entire class.[6] My classmates in that class came from African American, European American, and Hispanic American ethnic backgrounds. I cannot recall any of them commenting on my essay. To be quite honest, I sat stunned as my teacher read the words from the paper. Were they indeed my words? Yes, they were. God planted within me the gift of writing. My homeroom teacher, a European American who had earned her doctorate, congratulated me on the essay which was extra special because I had never met a teacher with a doctoral degree.

As a teenager, I spent many hours reading books in the quiet of my bedroom. My Dad blessed me with *Preparing for Adolescence: How to Survive the Coming Years of Change*, a book about godly sexuality and marriage for teenagers written by Dr. James Dobson of Focus on the Family.[7] It was not easy being a Christian, intelligent, brown-skinned African American girl in high school. White classmates said I was "not like the other black kids" most likely because they stereotyped black people as ignorant, poor, and violent. Some black students called me "white girl" because I made very good grades and liked learning. Some of my classmates believed the only way to be cool was to be sexually promiscuous. Others dressed provocatively like Hollywood celebrities and dancers in the new phenomena called music videos.

I read voraciously as a teenager. There were the classics assigned by my teachers. Some of the books I read included the ones on cooking and social etiquette from the public library. Oftentimes, they featured the story of African American leaders from the nineteenth century. I remember reading a huge volume with pictures about the beautiful, legendary Josephine Baker, and her bravery in finding freedom in France away from the racialized violence of the United States.

I read Richard Wright's *Native Son* and was gripped by Bigger's angry desperation in the novel set in Chicago.[8] How I relished Florida-born anthropologist-folklorist Zora Neale Hurston's novel, *Their Eyes Were Watching God*. I found similarity between the black people in Hurston's hometown Eatonville and my own. I studied details of her life in *Zora Neale Hurston: A Literary Biography* (1980) written by Robert E. Hemenway with a foreword by African American activist-writer Alice Walker.[10]

I also read several of Dr. Maya Angelou's riveting autobiographical accounts beginning with *I Know Why the Caged Bird Sings* (1970).[11] After celebrating with the Younger family who bought a decent house after living in the ghetto as depicted in Lorraine Hansberry's *A Raisin in the Sun*, I questioned silently the Duval County Schools curriculum.[12] There I was, a teenager in the newly integrated South, reading literature by African American writers independently, outside of the classroom. Why didn't Southern teachers assign work written by African Americans?

We did have a lesson on *To Kill a Mockingbird*, a novel with racial themes by Harper Lee (1960), a European American woman from Alabama.[13] However, it was not until my senior year in Advanced Placement that a single book written by an African American author was assigned. When my young, European American teacher announced that she wanted us to buy *Invisible Man*,[14] some (if not all) of the students who were all white save one Jewish girl thought she had assigned *The Invisible Man* (1897), the science fiction novel by H.G. Wells.[15] A collective groan went up when she clarified that we were going to read and discuss Ralph Ellison's *Invisible Man* (1952).[16] I decided that I liked African American literature and needed more to be prepared properly for college.

Sixteen

Being sixteen meant preparing to leave my father's house to go off to college. Colleges and universities from all over the United States—Carnegie Mellon, Hampton, Princeton, Stanford—sent me applications and brochures. The pictures of young adults from every major ethnic group sitting casually on campus conveyed that diversity was present and valued. Administrators seemed accessible and friendly as they explained why their institutions were the best. The majors offered showcased the various disciplines that would prepare students for careers after graduation.

Lush grass and tall, full trees beckoned to the nature lover in me as I tried to sort out which campus was my number one pick. The private schools seemed like the best, but their tuition and overall cost posed an obstacle for my family that had three children to educate. Thankfully, these institutions offered scholarships to talented students like me whose families had modest incomes.

I took the PSAT to get practice for the SAT and made a high score. A special prep course was offered to students of color who did well on the PSAT. Each week, I participated in the class that taught us how to focus on the questions we could answer while saving time by not getting stuck on questions that were more difficult. As a prize for our high scores, we were given tickets to see *Dreamgirls* at a local theatre.[17] It was a dazzling show and the first Broadway work I had ever seen.

My mother and I had a good time. One of my best friends had invited me to ask my mother about joining a local African American theater troupe for children and youth. Mama paid the fees so that I could study acting, dance, and music. My instructor loved children and really dedicated her life to presenting us with positive activities for our creative, young energy. At an afternoon performance the troupe did, I moved the audience and my instructor with my interpretation of Harlem Renaissance writer Langston Hughes' poem, "The Negro Mother."[18] I felt so happy that I was entertaining and made everyone proud. My interest in African American theater as a future scholar and teacher was birthed from this rich experience.

I worked as an assistant painter and a secretary for my Dad whose art studio was in the garage. Since I liked jewelry, I learned how to turn colorful beads into pretty bracelets and necklaces and sold them from a local beauty salon. After an interview at a department store fell through, I found a job at McDonald's as a cashier and a fry cook in a busy mall. It was a stressful time as my dear, sweet paternal aunt had died from complications of a failed suicide attempt. That summer I learned the value of a hard-earned dollar and of life which is priceless.

As a teenaged girl, I wanted to know more about becoming a woman. My Dad bought me a subscription to a magazine for teenaged girls. I read each issue and followed fashion on television on Saturday mornings. One summer, my mother enrolled me in a modeling school. I was given permission to wear makeup. We went shopping and found stylish clothing appropriate for a teenager. With the help of the staff photographer, I developed a portfolio of photographs. One teacher taught us about social etiquette. I modeled a beautiful turquoise gown at the graduation fashion show. After completing the class, I was a runway model for a charity to help abused children. Some time later, I did tearoom modeling for a sorority luncheon. I enjoyed feeling glamorous and serving God for worthy causes.

Seventeen

God blessed me to really focus and to make a high score on the SAT. I completed my homework assignments confident that I would be granted a scholarship to a top college or university. My dream was coming true.

My Father, Arrested?

Then my father was arrested. Two men came to the front door a short time after midnight demanding that he come with them to the police station. My mother begged him to take his car which he did. My senior class went to the park for lunch, and most of us wondered what awaited us after high school. We practiced for graduation night in the auditorium and then we returned to the campus. I asked one of my classmates to accompany me as I called my grandmother to tell her that my Dad was in jail. For the rest of the day, I was in shock.

Someone had created a black and white flyer featuring the pictures of several African American public figures on it that asked for their deaths in exchange for money. While my mother and I knew my father had not created the mean-spirited, sloppy flyer, we also knew that he had political enemies because of his outspokenness at city council meetings. My Dad knew that the county's schools lacked parity for poor children, and he was vocal about the decline in educational achievement.

The media descended upon our neighborhood, and asked neighbors what they knew. My mother protected my brothers and me as best she could. Students and teachers at school were talking about the case. My mother sought the best lawyer she could because of the severity of the charges. A few of the members of our church visited us and offered whatever they believed would console us at such a difficult time. My dream of attending college in the coming semester seemed to be impossible. Nonetheless, I walked across the stage on graduation night with my head held high. Two of my teachers consoled me and said that the truth would come out soon. I prayed that they were right.

That same summer, I had a corporate internship through INROADS, Inc. that helped me to develop great skills while making good money for college. My adviser was a parent with a Caribbean heritage, and believed in my ability to stretch and grow into a capable adult. INROADS, Inc. helped me to create my first résumé and career wardrobe. I applied the teachings my cohorts and I had been given on Saturdays in preparation for our interviews with companies for paid internships. God provided for me mightily by empowering me to land a position working at a major advertising agency. At the regional summer conference in Tampa, I stayed in a dormitory for the first time at the University of South Florida.

The Spelman Sisterhood: Blessings of Studying at a Black Women's College

*S*pelman College, "founded as Atlanta Female Seminary by Sophia B. Packard and Harriet E. Giles in 1881" with facilities "in [the] basement of Friendship Baptist Church, Reverend Frank Quarles, pastor," was my first choice school.[19] It was one of the colleges established to educate Black women in the United States. "Sophia B. Packard and Harriet E. Giles [were] schoolteachers and Baptist missionaries from New England" and each became presidents of Spelman which received philanthropic support from the Rockefellers.[20] The name "Spelman" comes from "Mrs. Laura Spelman Rockefeller and her parents Buel and Lucy Henry Spelman, longtime activists in the antislavery movement."[21]

Perhaps because I had been one of the few students of color in my advanced high school classes, I applied to historically black colleges and universities (HBCUs) where I felt I would among true scholars. I wanted to be around young people who were like me. One of the most painful experiences that any African American student in school can experience is to be called "white" because he or she is intelligent. I wanted to feel like I was part of a vibrant community that cared about improving and serving African Americans. Both of my parents took classes at HBCUs as young adults. God blessed me to be accepted by Spelman College.

I believe that practicing good habits during the first year of college positions students for lifelong success. Day by day, the Lord God blessed me to prioritize pleasing Him by concentrating on mastering the academic material before me and making good grades. That first semester, I woke up each morning and prayed beside my twin bed in the room I shared with two other young women at Spelman College. A postcard from one of them before enrollment was my introduction before my mother drove me and my Grandmama north of Jacksonville to Atlanta to move me into Abbey Hall.

Instead of staying in the hotel with my family, I slept in the dormitory; my room adjacent to the residential hall assistant's room. Balmy with the perfumed scent of magnolia trees, the Spelman campus was a beautiful place where black women from all over the world have earned degrees. I have never felt as safe anywhere as I did at Spelman. The security guards were actually police officers who treated us like royalty, protecting us from predators, and university students from the other schools. Our school's mission of centered on offering us the best education possible.

As I made friends with other young women that weekend, I did not focus so much on the hellish weeks that preceded my reaching my destination. All I knew was that God had shown me how good He is and what great things He had planned for my life in spite of my parents' problems.

I met a warm, coffee-colored sister from New York who wore here hair in a curly perm during Orientation Week, and we became close friends. We let loose and laughed at the Six Flags Amusement Park where the school treated us to a day of fun during Orientation Week. My dear Spelman sister's sunny disposition and street smarts as a child of Jamaica helped me to navigate social events during that first homecoming week, and to dodge dangerous men who tried to threaten us on our own campus. I had never seen condoms until they threw them from the balcony at the Manley Student Center one Friday afternoon. I felt insulted by the suggestion that godly women like us—of every hue of beautiful black, and intelligent—would want anything to do with such callous creatures.

Getting up to enjoy a simple breakfast of juice and cereal or hot grits and eggs each morning, I met my friends in the cafeteria in the Manley Center, and started the day grateful and hopeful for the future. Getting the most out of my college experience required discipline, and a willingness to be use my intelligence and uniqueness so I could be the best student I could be. During the first few weeks, I had the wisdom to request a room change just before my two roommates lost their visiting privileges.

My third roommate was a quiet, sweet, lemon drop-colored young woman from Beverly Hills. She borrowed my TV to watch *90210*. It was the first time she'd lived in a predominantly black environment and seemed to like it, and I had never met anyone from Beverly Hills. We got along well.

My first semester at Spelman included a world history course taught by a renowned African American scholar. We were entranced by his dark, handsome, movie star looks, and often remarked to each other how much he reminded us of our fathers and actor Denzel Washington. He grew up in a single-parent home in Chicago and earned his history degree at the prestigious University of Chicago. He taught about global events and people of the past from a perspective that was inclusive and respected our African beginnings.

When I visited his office, the spunky voice of the jazz singer Dinah Washington welcomed me. I asked him who was singing, not knowing that his answer would propel me to invest in classic and modern jazz albums and cassettes until I had been re-educated about the role of African American women and popular music. The African calendar on my professor's wall and the shelves of unending books reminded me of my Dad's home library which included a set of *EBONY* Magazine published by the legendary Mr. John H. Johnson.[22] How I loved sitting in the front of the class and raising my hand to be called upon to join the discussion! What safety I felt in his office confiding that, saddened by Dad being held as a political prisoner in my formerly Jim Crow hometown in Florida, I knew I needed to be at Spelman getting a degree to help make things right in a troubled world.

A Christian man with a wife and daughters, my professor was also a favorite of male student leaders studying across the street from Spelman at Morehouse College. The esteemed institution where Dr. Martin Luther King, Jr.[23] had excelled under the tutelage of Dr. Benjamin Mays.[24] Mays led the global peace movement against European colonialism through nonviolent protest and stood tall as a living monument to black male achievement. Two of my friends, one from North Carolina and the other from Texas, and I went there to worship occasionally on Sunday mornings. Stepping carefully to avoid the beer cans and glass strewn in the parking lot from the night before, we sat in awe of the speakers who included the chaplain, a Gospel rapper, and clergy from Ebenezer Baptist Church.[25]

It was not so hard to not be promiscuous in an environment like the Atlanta University Center.[26] We were *chosen*, and God made a way for us to grow up into young adults without taking our clothes off to impress others. Instead, we donned our thinking caps daily, asking questions in class and spending time at the Woody Library we shared with five historically black colleges and universities. Named after Robert W. Woodruff, the philanthropist, the media center served primarily as a reading hub where we found our professors had given assignments for us to find on reserve.[27] Intrigued by the aged books from yesteryear and the culturally astute librarians, I loved venturing through the neighborhood of small, modest homes and culturally conscious street art to Woody Library to learn how to honor my legacy using my mind.

Getting the Most out of College

Getting the most out of my college experience required discipline and a willingness to be different. My daily routine during the school week helped to secure my success. I prayed before I left my room for myself and for my Dad. My *Holy Bible* functioned as my wisest friend. God answered my prayer regarding my Dad early in September, when God used a sharp lawyer and a compassionate judge to free my father from jail. He accompanied the entire family to visit me at school around the time of my eighteenth birthday.

After a shower and getting dressed, I ate breakfast every morning at Manley Center with my friends to give myself the energy for the day's classes. I tried to be a few minutes early, I took detailed notes, and participated by asking and answering questions in every class. Completing my homework was a top priority for me each evening and on the weekend. Not all of my friends had been blessed to attend their top pick school so I knew it was up to me to make the most of this golden opportunity. I did not sleep around. I did not cheat and I did not curse. My diligence paid off when I was inducted into the honor society and received a scholarship from the honors program in my sophomore year.

In college, it is important to find something to do when you are not in class. During Homecoming Weekend, campus performers presented a play that I had co-written with other Spelman women. Many other student organizations existed on campus. I chose to work on the newspaper and yearbook staffs at Spelman since I like to write. It was fun to work alongside other Spelman women in student media. I heard noted writers lecture about hip hop music and reaching out to women in prison. Occasionally, I took an afternoon nap or my friends and I would go shopping at the mall. On Friday or Saturday nights, we danced with handsome college men or in one large, pulsating body of rhythm at Manley Center or Morehouse. Successful students are balanced students.

As a child in Florida, I had been introduced to swimming at the YMCA. My skill level improved during the class I enrolled in at Spelman to satisfy the physical education requirement. Because I was learning new strokes, some evenings, I went to the pool to practice swimming techniques with my classmates. Through the teaching of my pregnant swimming instructor and hours of practice, I finally learned to swim.

As a sophomore, I moved into another dorm and had my own room. Most of the students who lived there were upper class-women in their latter years of study. In my last year at Spelman, I spent more time with older students in the Department of English. In one course on non-fiction writing by nineteenth century African American women writers, I was the only under class-woman enrolled.

During one assignment, we researched homelessness in Atlanta. I went to my professor during her office hours and spoke openly about my sense that my classmates did not respect my opinion. A dark-skinned, petite woman with impeccable English and a wealth of knowledge about writers of color, she understood the situation and reassured me that I was bright and in the right place. However, it was while completing a biographical paper on Dr. Anna Julia Heyward Cooper, the daughter of an enslaved African woman and a white man who wrote *A Voice from the South* (1892) and founded a university, that I learned the value of listening to my more mature Spelman sisters.[29] My report was videotaped. In her evaluation of our group project, my professor pointed out errors and strengths, and my classmates and I discussed our grade. After this experience, I longed for more in-depth research opportunities.

Discovering the Third World:
Scholarship at Oberlin College

After an official from Belize gave a talk to my honors class at Spelman, my mind began to wonder about life in other countries. I wanted to compete for research grants to find the answers to intellectual questions. How was my mother going to afford to send both of my brothers to college and me overseas? I talked to people I trusted at Spelman about my dilemma and decided to apply to two other private colleges as a transfer student. A kind alumna gave me a good reference for Oberlin College where the financial aid officer awarded me a generous package. My mother bought me winter boots which I needed for the heavy snow in Ohio. I moved into the Afrikan Heritage House designed to immerse residents in African Diasporan cultural events. Over the course of the first week, I met other transfer students from around the world and spent time with them during orientation.

During the first semester, I took an English literature course that was unlike all others I had ever taken. My professor was from India, and she had earned her doctorate in the United States. In her class, we read African, African American, British, and Caribbean literature. Topics we studied included anti-slavery movements, feminism, and post-colonialism. For the first time, I was consciously reading and discussing literature in English written by people of color. When I went to my professor's office, she was warm and encouraged me to continue my studies.

I admired my professor and decided to enroll in whatever class she was teaching for upper-classmen. During this time in my career, she introduced me to the term "Anglophonic" which means "written in English." My classmates and I read and discussed literature written by African American, Asian, British, and Caribbean writers including Edward Said.[30] It was a lesson on Mary Shelley's novel, *Frankenstein, or The Modern Prometheus* (1818) that really convinced me of the value of the Third World feminist point of view.[31]

Like many Americans, I had seen the most famous black and white *Frankenstein* movie.[32] It scared me because of the demonic desire of Dr. Frankenstein and the horrible creature he had invented from parts of human beings. The brilliance of my professor's teaching was conveyed in her beautiful cottage over a home-cooked, Indian meal. She suggested that Shelley's gothic novel could be read through a Third World feminist lens. The monster Dr. Frankenstein created threatened the Europeans in the village, heightened by the scene in which he accidentally kills Maria.

Beyond the hideous Frankenstein existed the possibility that he was another breed of human—a non-white, superhuman breed of human. In the colorful home of an Indian American woman scholar, and her European American husband who taught at a community college, I imagined a life as a successful academic. I saw an even softer side of my professor as a mother when her two cute, brown-skinned, young sons came into the room. I felt inspired by my professor's ability to weave hospitality with intellectualism. She explored feminist texts but did not degrade men in front of students. "I want to be that happy when I grow up," I said to myself.

Since this memorable time, I moved forward in my studies and traveled to England in the United Kingdom.

Living in London

By the end of my first year at Oberlin, God had blessed me to be an Andrew Mellon Minority Fellow with an approved project in modern African American literature. I had the extraordinary experience of being selected to act in an ensemble cast doing scenes from plays by Adrienne Kennedy, an African American playwright. Our professor, a confident, sweet African American woman who studied theatre at Yale University, brought me and two of my classmates from the Afrikan Heritage House together for rehearsals. "The Theater Program at Oberlin began in the 1970s, but performing arts of all kinds have been an integral part of Oberlin's history since the college was founded in 1833."[33]

For one play, I recruited a male friend from the Philippines for the role of Jesus. During the annual Great Lakes Theatre Festival, we performed scenes on race, class, sex, art, and religion at Case Western University, a local library, and finally at Oberlin. I met actress Ruby Dee the night of the premiere of Kennedy's play, *Ohio State Murders* (1992).[34] My classmates and I also met the playwright and her son at the after party.

Oberlin professors nominated me because of my major and maturity to travel to England with about 29 other students through the Danenberg-in-London Program. Our trip began in the winter of 1993 when the IRA bombings were common. Being in a foreign country that influenced so much of my own land's beginnings was a once-in-a-lifetime experience. During the morning, I studied Shakespearean drama and modern literature with a professor from Oberlin's Department of English. I ate lunch like fish and chips and Mediterranean fare and went shopping with my classmates in the afternoon. Several evenings during the month, we went to the theater to see the plays we had read. My college education afforded me the opportunity to go to shows at the Barbican, to see plays performed by the Royal Shakespeare Company. A few times we attended dance concerts and the opera. We read W. H. Auden[35] and T.S. Eliot and viewed modern art at the Tate.

An independent research project required that each of us explore a special aspect of the UK. Having grown up in Florida, I had many neighbors from the Caribbean and decided to investigate this culture's presence in British society. I chose to interview a black British DJ about the country's love of Caribbean and American Soul music, and enjoyed live concerts with a Caribbean-born classmate and new friends. Many people assumed I was from the Caribbean until they heard my American accent.

Posters of beautiful, black supermodel Naomi Campbell were plastered all over the city. When the Indian roommate of a Caribbean-born fellow insisted he needed to see popular filmmaker Spike Lee's *Malcolm X* movie, my new Caribbean female friend helped me to not make a huge mistake by accepting his invitation. I thanked him for his valor, having already danced with the smooth, brown-skinned D. J. at a small nightclub.

My friend was raised in Trinidad and I enjoyed a delicious meal from her country called saltfish and ackee with curried meat with rice as we agreed to celebrate the ability and the willingness to care and to share across national boundaries. One day I listened to black British editor Margaret Busby read poetry from

Daughters of Africa (1992) and attended a Third World book fair and forum with exiled and popular writers of color.[39] It was fun to buy black books and to meet living literary and music legends like Linton Kwesi Johnson.[40]

Many black cultural events were held in Brixton which was not far from our student house in Vauxhall. Two black British publishers introduced me to *O.P.P.* by Naomi King, a novel influenced by the American hip hop tune, and I read it hungrily from cover to cover. I treated myself by getting my haired styled in African braids by my Caribbean classmate and a stylist from Guyana. Sundays, I worshipped at multicultural churches although I found it sad how few churches exist in the country in comparison to pubs. I ventured to find black British cultural events on my own since they had not been factored into our program despite my sharing with my European American professor at the beginning of the semester that this was something I thought he should be aware of.

Near the end of my trip, I enjoyed the "foremost black-led" Talawa Theatre Company's production of Dr. Endesha Ida Mae Holland's autobiographical play *From the Mississippi Delta*. It was Holland's 1984 memoirs and the details her life in Mississippi during the modern civil rights movement.[42] Of the importance of identity, she writes, "A child does not need to dwell in her mother's house to be a loyal daughter, I realized, or stay in her birthplace to remember where she's from."[43]

Interestingly enough, the actress who portrayed Holland also starred in the color blind version of William Shakespeare's *The Two Gentlemen of Verona* (1598).[44] "[David] Thacker's 1991 production of *The Two Gentlemen of Verona*, was set in the effete social world of the thirties among the bright young things of the salon society. The Milan Court became a party in an English country house."[45] Additionally, Thacker's production of what is believed to be Shakespeare' first play had a jazzy mood with "songs by Cole Porter, Irving Berlin and the Gershwins."[46] The black actress sang beautifully wearing a lovely gown. Her flexibility in speaking both in British English and in Southern Black English was admirable and a little humorous.

For spring break, I took a solo day trip to Oxford and found it to be a quaint university town. On another afternoon, a Christian European American classmate and I decided to take a bus trip to Cambridge. An IRA bombing of London's financial district redirected our route, but we reached our destination and had a good time. We took pictures of Cambridge University, saw a newly married Asian couple in the park, and indulged in chocolate truffles from a chocolatier. I found it easy to relate to people of different ethnicities during my trip to the UK. Truly, people of the African Diaspora have been very adaptable in the Western world. I returned to the United States grateful for the blessings that we have materially, but also convinced of the similarity of people's basic needs for freedom, good health and love.

Survivor Story

My First Kiss

I was the only woman at the table. The men spoke passionately about academia, the economy, and politics over wings and drinks. The sun had set a few hours earlier. He studied mathematics and was gentleman enough to walk me back to the clubhouse where our colleagues were playing pool and watching TV. The night air was perfect as I breathed in its freshness from the front steps. One of my colleague's friends came by and told me that he would be with me in a few minutes.

Sure enough, several inches taller than me with dark chocolate skin and short locs, he appeared. We walked to his dorm and then something unexpectedly lovely happened. From the highest point of the building we were in, you could see the indigo mountains and thick forests. It was like we were in a gazebo in the sky. He pointed out the nature around us, but I was following the deep, soft signals in his voice. Then he reached for my hand. As he massaged the second one, he drew me close to him and then lifted my chin until our lips met: "Let him kiss me with the kisses of his mouth—for

46

your love is better than wine," I thought, recalling Song of Solomon 1:2.

Time became endless as we embraced. My colleague walked me back to the clubhouse and to my room where my best friend was still awake. I said good night and slept peacefully. It was all like the sweetest dream, only the kiss had been real.

My First Boyfriend

Like many immigrant men, this man believed that all American women are promiscuous, rich, and sexually available. Like many of my African American women classmates, I was lonely, wanted to date and have fun. At that time, Oberlin was a campus where there were few African American men and numerable bisexual and gay male students. I wanted to marry one day and have a family. With blueberry black skin and bittersweet memories of his African homeland, my first boyfriend was something of a father figure. He said he saw me and thought I was "cute," and his condescending behavior proved that he did not take me seriously.

Divorced and the father of one son, my first boyfriend and I met on a campus in Ohio. He was a scholar completing his dissertation, and I was a senior applying to graduate school while making plans for a career in publishing. At first, I felt relieved to meet someone who was not bisexual or gay as a significant number of the male population at Oberlin were at that time. My boyfriend rented part of a house and had no problem taking me out to dinner or the movies away from the sleepy town destined to be my alma mater. He gave me flowers once or twice, but my favorite gift from him was a stylish pen. I appreciated the fact that he acknowledged my desire to have a career as a writer. He gave me tips on getting manuscripts done that I remember to this day. We cooked pasta together and had dinner with my trusted group of friends twice.

Unfortunately, my first boyfriend was raised in a Muslim, polygamous household. My angst at not being part of a couple with a decent, Christian young man in my peer group got the best of me. My first boyfriend never spoke of *The Holy Quaran* or going to the mosque although he did have a prayer mat.[47] However, even though he was in his late thirties, the hurt he experienced from a strained relationship with his father was quite evident. Additionally, he expressed his disdain for the polygamous lifestyle.

An honors student with my entire future ahead of me, I was simply happy to have someone, a male companion, to spend time with, to talk to. I had experienced my first kiss only a few short weeks before I started dating my first boyfriend. I liked being 21. My boyfriend's sexual appetite and experience were two areas that I had underestimated, and I found that I was not exactly safe with him.

After the staged reading of scenes from my first play, *Indigo Prayer*, I walked over to my boyfriend's place to share with him the details of the successful production. He was busy working on his dissertation that evening but welcomed me in. It was barely an hour later that I stood in the bathroom crying, my sweater lifted above my head to expose the pretty, satin bra my mother had bought me. There were times when my boyfriend and I argued because I did not want to have sex before I was married. He would offer to sleep with other women and have me on the side, but I told him no deal—we could just part ways.

His fingers and mouth on my body felt cold and creepy, and it took many, many years before I told a rape hotline counselor what had happened. On a night when I wanted my man to share in my success, all I got was violation and ugly words about Mary, the mother of Jesus Christ. I had one friend who understood what I was going through as she also had an older, more established boyfriend, a campus staff member, who took advantage of her. Then she found out his fiancé lived in another country.

Shortly after that horrible night, I was shocked to discover that I had not been granted admission to any of the graduate school programs I had submitted applications to for the following year. Had I spent so much time being an angry man's girlfriend that I had not paid enough attention to my own future? As I have matured as a Christian and listened to and read other women's survivor stories, I have come to realize that the devil is not my friend.

On the contrary, it is Jesus Christ who calls church members friends: "No longer do I call you servants, for a servant does not know what his master is doing; but I have called you friends, for all things that I heard from My Father I have made known to you" (John 15:15).

After I stopped having anything to do with my ex-boyfriend, I applied myself to the final semester of my studies at Oberlin. In the spring, I was the only African American student inducted into Phi Beta Kappa, the national honor society.

The Day Grandmama Came North

My maternal grandmother is a beautiful, Bible-believing, humble, giving woman. She helped my young mother to care for us which allowed Mama to find the time to study for and enter a career as a registered nurse. Grandmama served many European American families as a domestic worker for many years. I listen to her stories of the days when that was the main occupation for millions of African American women and wondered how they did it. Racial inequality was the rule in the South, the wages were low, and circumstances often meant that the worker would go from family to family with no pension in sight. In later life, my grandmother was blessed with a job in a local hospital. She retired after several years of service with a pension and a newfound pride.

Grandmama was born in the twenties and came from a small town in Georgia. Her father and mother worked hard to provide for their children. Grandmama's mother was African American and American Indian and died in her thirties when my grandmother was a girl. Through godly living including loving kindness towards me and instruction on staying close to God, Grandmama embodied wisdom: "Length of days is at her right hand, in her left hand riches and honor....She is a tree of life to those who take hold of her, and happy are all who retain her" (Proverbs 3:16, 18).

My grandmother had never traveled as far North as Ohio. I was looking forward to celebrating my academic accomplishments with my loved ones. After my Dad arrived and spent time with me, my mother, grandmother, and one of my younger brothers came to Oberlin. Dad introduced me to an aunt whose home was in Ohio. It felt like a family reunion. Even though I learned that weekend that my parents were going through a divorce, I was grateful to God that they made an appearance out of love to me.

The Department of Black Studies had a tradition of engraving words of thanks on a plaque for each graduate for participation in the Black Parent Appreciation Program. After the Mistress of Ceremony read the message I had written to my family, Grandmama and the rest of my family stood to receive the plaque and flowers I had bought. In the four years that I had been away from Florida studying for my degree, I had never felt so thankful to God for the gift of family.

From Ohio to New York

*T*he summer after I graduated from college, I started applying for jobs in the publishing industry in New York. Oddly, I had not been accepted into any of the graduate school programs I had applied to before the spring. Moreover, my parents did not relate to me well as a college graduate. There was no discussion of my dreams and careers goals even though I had made it to the top of my class, but they did make it clear that I was expected to return to Florida. I chose my own dream: "When my father and my mother forsake me, then the Lord will take care of me" (Psalm 27:10).

I decided that working in publishing would be a good thing to do since I had studied English, was a writer in college, and hoped to become an editor one day. During most of the summer, I conducted research on modern African American writers for my fellowship at Oberlin. Most of the rest of the time was devoted to an active job search. One company sent a rejection letter. The others did not bother to contact me at all. One of the staff members in the career services office put me in touch with his daughter who was working in publishing at the time. She gave me some pointers and talked about what to expect if I did land a job as an editorial assistant. I browsed a volume on jobs for creative people and searched the internship section, but knew that working for free was out of the question.

Finally, I landed an interview with a popular, liberal weekly magazine often used by college professors. I received notification that I had been selected as a candidate and arranged a telephone interview. The morning of the interview, I dressed up professionally and was asked questions over the telephone by one of the people who I would be reporting to if I landed the paid internship. A short time after the interview, the company informed me that I had been chosen out of 500 applicants for the position. I was so happy I would be living and working in New York!

Once I had work, I started thinking about housing. One of my professor's mother lived in a complex operated by the Salvation Army. I contacted the office to see if they had anything available for someone like me, and they did. The staff placed me on a waiting list for the Evangeline Markle, a high rise complex in the West Village exclusively for women who were students or working, and senior citizens of both genders. During my undergraduate years, I had traveled to New York with a classmate and friend to conduct research at places including the Arthur Schomburg Center.[48] However, I had not ever lived in New York. How was I going to be able to make the transition into the real world? Living biblically by reading *The Holy Bible*, abstaining from alcohol, drugs, and sex, and avoiding strange environments gave me a good measure of safety.

When I traveled from Ohio to New York, I was not alone; a friend who was in the class before mine and I decided to go to the big city together. We had completed a course on the American church taught by a Baptist woman minister one semester as well. My friend was Catholic, and her family in Kentucky had done a favor for some priests. In turn, we were given room and board by nuns in New York right in the middle of Harlem. They were the friendliest, most kind nuns I had ever met. In their senior years, most of them had taken their vows as teenagers. I felt safe in the convent but knew my stay there was temporary. A tall, dark-skinned nun asked me to stay, saying I would not find anything outside of its walls, but I was determined to see for myself.

During the day, my friend and I walked through the West Village. She found a job in a shoe store. I was on the waiting list for a space at the Salvation Army Evangeline Markle Residence. Two of the nuns passed away while we were at the convent, so the sisters split us up to make room for the families coming in for the funeral arrangements. Briefly, I stayed with a nice family the nuns knew in Queens.

In a short time, a space opened up at the Evangeline Markle. I shared a nice, furnished room with three other young women. We had a bathroom, closets, and maid service. Good meals were served three times a day during the week. The lovely building had a lobby where male company could be received. Men were not allowed in our rooms. We shared two television rooms, one with cable TV and one with a big screen. By the time I had started my internship, I was settled into my room nicely.

The office was within walking distance of where I lived, and I had time to return to the Evangeline Markle for dinner. I assisted the literary editor who allowed me to pick out and keep whatever review copies of new books I wanted. Additionally, I served in the circulation department and made press releases. The strongest taste

I had of true journalism came when I worked as a fact-checker for a veteran newsman on a story about Haiti.

My six other colleagues and I made it through three months of full-time, fast-paced, investigative work for seventy-five dollars a week. I exercised restraint financially by reserving my credit card for two purchases: a blue cardigan and a ticket to hear *Sweet Honey in the Rock* at Carnegie Hall. Initially, my mother and grandmother sent me kind, cash gifts a few times. However, by finding a part-time job as a bookseller at Barnes and Noble, I was able to maintain my independence. God provided everything for my survival as a young adult in the big city just as Paul wrote in Philippians 4:19:

"And my God shall supply all your need according to His riches in glory by Christ Jesus."

One evening, I received a phone call from one of my favorite writers. I shared with her my love of her work which emphasizes the African continuity in African American and Caribbean literature. After I named the graduate school programs I was considering, she made some suggestions. I felt so happy because a previous letter I had written to her after I had done a report on one of her novels in high school had been returned. It was hard to believe that it was so easy to get in contact with famous writers, but in New York, they lived throughout the city.

After graduating from college, I sought examples of successful Black women for inspiration. Dr. Johnnetta B. Cole, Spelman's first Black woman President, wrote a book that broadened my vision of what I could accomplish in life entitled *Conversations: Straight Talk with America's Sister President* (1994). This was the most important book I have ever read about education, gender, race, and successful futures for African American women. It is a candid account of her own journey as a college student from Fisk University, an HBCU in Tennessee to Oberlin College in Ohio. Cole, who comes from an influential family in Jacksonville, Florida, also shares the story of her talented sister, a musician. After graduation, Cole and her European American class-mate lived as husband and wife, parenting children in Africa. She analyzes the challenges African American families face due to the high rates of African American male incarceration and the drug trade. Connecting her own story of being an anthropologist, a wife, a mother, and educator, she presents the myriad of possibilities for a new generation of black women.

God gave me favor with a frank, giving African American woman writer and teacher who made it clear to me that my mind could change the world. She completed her first book as a teenager, but faced opposition from older black women writers for the way in which she took on racism and sexism in America. I was one of the few students to excel in a course she taught on African American women writers at Oberlin. She helped me to make a connection to move to the next level as a literature scholar.

A graduate of one of her courses, a kind, African American professor and his trustworthy African American female colleague assisted me in finding the university teacher training program that was best for me. In declaring her dismay at the lack of women teachers in my family, my mentor's colleague helped me to put my knowledge of biology, commerce, and linguistics into practice academically. My black feminist professor wrote me such a powerful reference letter that

I was offered admittance into several top universities. I decided to attend the University of Maryland, College Park where I received a fellowship to study English.

Making Black Books Real: Teaching

*B*eing a black woman word warrior is my destiny. I love being a writer, but it has come with a high price. After college, my father attacked me in letters, criticizing me for leaving the South and living in New York. My mother attacked me physically in her apartment after I received a Ph.D. fellowship award letter from the Department of English from the University of Maryland, College Park.

A walk in the misty rain refreshed my soul as I considered my future. *I am going to become a college professor*, I thought while listening to music on my walkman. When I arrived back at my mother's apartment, she and my youngest brother who was also visiting that summer, were watching a religious program on TV. I spoke to them and went into the study that had been converted to my bedroom, and changed into a Hollywood-style nightgown my grandmother had given me. I felt tired and needed to rest. Before napping, I talked to one of my best friends on the phone.

A discerning, Christian woman whose father was a minister, she gasped and told me that my mother was jealous of me. I hung up the phone and reached for a book designed to guide women of color and decided to read a little of it. My mother started banging on the door and saying, "Veronica, open the door. No one is going to hurt you. Open the door."

Though it sounded like the climax of a horror movie, I obediently opened the door. My mother blocked the doorway with her body and began to threaten me. "I am going to get you some help!" she yelled before jumping on top of me. Her nearly three hundred pounds made me feel like I was suffocating. I reached for the phone next to me. Seeing what I was doing, she jumped up off of me and raced to her bedroom next door and called some hotline.

I spoke to the kind woman who answered my call. She asked whether or not I could go and live with my father. I told her that my parents were going through a bitter divorce and that I would go to stay with my grandmother. Within half an hour, I had packed a few large suitcases and was at the bus stop to ride to meet my grandmother. She opened her home to me, but for the rest of the summer my mother made appearances, perhaps to let me know that she had control. *She was wrong.* God was in control and would get me through even of the suffering that was to come.

Such dysfunction was not at all what I had expected in the weeks before I was scheduled to embark on my journey to become the first woman doctor of *anything* in my family. The night before my father and I were scheduled to ride the bus to Maryland, he took me to dinner and told me, "*You are chosen.*" We saw a late showing of the movie *The Net* at the mall.[49] Afterwards, between leaving the theatre and arriving back at my grandmother's apartment complex, I had two anxiety attacks. Even though I nearly fainted twice, no one—not the police officer or movie staff in the mall, not my father, not my grandmother—called the paramedics at 9-1-1.

The next day, my grandmother rode to church with my mother, telling me to rest and to not let anyone in the apartment. Grandmama's male friend came by, but, obediently, I did not let him in. I could tell my grandmother was worried about what had happened because she called me about every ten minutes. I started weeping. As I made my way to Grandmama's mirror, I remembered being wounded by the Muslim in Ohio.

Anxiety Attack!

I felt a strange, super strong force propel me all the way out of the apartment to the fourth floor balcony that I had never been on before. I hit the wall with both hands which prevented my jumping over and spoke about how God does not want us to be ashamed of our bodies. Several church women dressed in white came to my side and said my words were true and asked where my clothes were. They took me back to my grandmother's apartment where I put on a white dress. Two policemen arrived, one black, one white. The black one said he did not see any problem. The white officer put me in handcuffs and raced me to a private, behavioral health hospital on the other side of town. A blonde, European American woman did the intake, asking me where I was going. I told her the University of Maryland and then I was led to a room and instructed to get rest.

The Hispanic American doctor only called me to his office once. He laughed the entire time, but told my mother that the diagnosis was bipolar disorder. During the outpatient treatment, I met with a social worker who was also Hispanic. She and the doctor told my mother I would not be able to go to school for at least a year. Several times while I was working my own way towards becoming a writer, my mother lamented how she had dreamed of studying English and how following that path had been dashed.

I knew a year in Jacksonville would be unbearable. My future awaited me in Maryland. The African American dietician told my father that he felt concerned because I was not eating. Dad bought me some hot wings, and my appetite perked up. Through art therapy, I imagined myself walking out of the door, a hat on my head, and a stack of books in my hands.

My vision became reality the day my Dad and I boarded the bus for Maryland. When we arrived at the Department of English, a staff person smiled and said how wonderful it was that my father had come with me. Yes, how wonderful indeed! I found a compassionate, Indian American woman doctor who prescribed medication and advised me on foods to eat, and a European American man who practiced psychology. My thesis adviser is top in the field. I felt that God had trusted me with so much by allowing me to study and to write under her tutelage. In two years, I graduated with an "A" average and a master's degree in English Language and Literature.

Near the end of my program of study at the University of Maryland, College Park, the Department of English offered me a golden opportunity to teach undergraduate students. One of my colleagues needed to tend to another facet of her degree program, and there was a spot open to cover her class. With several courses on my transcript and a liberal arts degree with honors in Black Studies, I was chosen for the part.

It was an incredible semester. The course, "Introduction to African American Literature," was an elective taken by students who were in various majors and different levels of study. The class was diverse and large in size. I started the semester with African cosmology, the idea of being, and "*nommo*," the word."[50] At Oberlin, an African professor gave a lecture about nommo which is "a concept of the language of the Dogon" as we studied Janheinz Jahn's important study *Muntu: African Culture and the Western World.*[51] The popular book was originally published in 1961 and was reintroduced in 1989.

As a Christian, I pointed to John's definition of the word in the opening chapter of his gospel: "In the beginning was the Word, and the Words was with God, and the Word was God." Some of my students were familiar with this Bible verse. We discussed the autobiographical *The Narrative of the Life of Frederick Douglass* (1845).[52] We covered the period after slavery, writing of the late nineteenth century, with the class being assigned to go and see the John Singleton Hollywood film *Rosewood* (1997) about a prosperous African American community attacked by a white lynch mob in Florida.[53] Some students knew about the Harlem Renaissance which is a period that many instructors focus on for its vibrant quality and the many different authors who wrote during it. The World War II era with its modern texts and then the Black Power Movement poetry of the 1960s were new to many of the students.[54]

Most of the young adults in the survey course I taught on the African American literary tradition had no formal introduction to or training in it, although some of them had done reading on their own. As an undergraduate at Spelman College, I was taught by writers from this culture and others who visited the Atlanta University Center to share their perspectives and wisdom with us. Other renowned African American writers were my professors when I studied at Oberlin in the Midwest. My degree program was very rich on both campuses, and for this I am very thankful because it made me better prepared as a college instructor.

We had a fun lesson on writing by Zora Neale Hurston, the anthropologist-writer who studied Black folk in her native Florida, New York, and the Caribbean. We read aloud some of her creations so students could hear the African American vernacular, or Black English, and see it written on the page phonetically.[55] At the end of the term, we watched LeRoi Jones' play, *Dutchman*, on video and discussed its provocative look at race, sex, and violence.[56] It was important for me to make the literature come alive using technology for students preparing to enter a more complex work world.

I learned from experienced faculty how to navigate challenging classroom situations. Because of my young age and gender, a few African American women students tested me. They talked loudly in threatening voices and demanded top grades when they had not earned them. I remained in control of my classroom, using the techniques I had seen my more effective professors employ. I was not a barely clad video dancer, but a well-educated college literature instructor at a Research University. The students who doubted that someone my age, color, and sex could teach in college saw the reality of it all confirmed when they received their grades.

American students need to experience having college instructors and professors who defy the stereotype of the middle-aged white man in a light blue cardigan. Most of the world is made of women and girls of color whose first language is not English. By not backing down and expecting the best from my students, I earned their respect and taught them to take the development of their minds seriously by reading and writing in preparation for their classes and, ultimately, college graduation. In two years, I gained new knowledge, served students as a teacher, and graduated with an "A" average and a master's degree in English Language and Literature. On graduation day, my mother smiled with pride, and I was happy that she was there.

When I had attended family reunions on my maternal grandmother's side of the family when I was younger, my relatives commented on my intelligence. Because my favorite male cousin and I were so gifted, the family believed that we would both go to college. We started our postsecondary academic careers at historically black colleges and universities commonly known as HBCUs. Studies prove that most African Americans who go on to earn doctoral degrees and who become professionals begin their college educations at HBCUs.[57] At one reunion, one of my great aunt's sons sat beside me and told me that he wanted his daughters to be just like me. Truthfully, I was caught unawares. You never know who is watching you. I am a role model in my family:

"Teach me, O Lord, the way of Your statutes, And I shall keep it to the end. Give me understanding, and I shall keep Your law; Indeed, I shall observe it with my whole heart" (Psalm 119:33-34).

Many of my female cousins became mothers as teenagers without wedding rings on their fingers. Perhaps their poor choices were due to the poor examples they were given by their parents, and a lack of exposure to healthier lifestyles outside of their communities. A few of my female cousins enlisted in the military and got married. Others attended community college and a small percentage graduated from four-year colleges. My cousin and I graduated with honors from college and earned fellowships and graduate degrees before teaching at the college level. We continue to attend family reunions whenever we can out of devotion for our ancestors and loved ones.

Being in the Big Apple

*B*eing in the Big Apple, New York City, was an answered prayer. As a young adult who had been an editor and a writer in college, I thanked God for making a way for me to live and to work in the place where so many writers and other artists had been successful. While serving as an editor-indexer for the National Trust Library for Historic Preservation housed at the University of Maryland, I gained meaningful experience for my future career. I created entries from articles on historic preservation of buildings for the electronic library catalog system. It was a blessing to be both in graduate school and in an environment where my writing gift proved useful.

My supervisor encouraged me and gave me a copy of Fodor's *New York* after I shared that I was leaving Maryland to join my fiancé. We met in late June at the Mellon conference hosted in Hampton, Virginia. It is funny how I was sad at first because a black Latino colleague from Harvard who I had been corresponding with did not show up and sent a message by another woman. I saw my future husband standing by the lake and introduced myself. I was wearing a little red dress and ruby heels. The moonlight made his dark eyes shine as he told me his name. We danced then went for a walk on the beach. I accompanied him to his room, feeling giddy, and nervous. He quietly described himself as "Mexican" as I said timidly, "I have African American lips." For some time, we kissed in the small room while many of our colleagues below watched the brutal Mike Tyson vs. Evander Holyfield boxing match. Before we parted that weekend, we exchanged email addresses.

My first love had more sexual experience than me. I was a virgin in my twenties. Unfortunately, he came from an environment where rich white men often exploited Hispanic boys and men for work and for sex. As a teenager, my boyfriend had worked on a ranch. His European American male high school teacher, seeing that a positive male role model was missing from his life, mentored him. He enrolled in a top liberal arts college in New England. It was a new, wealthier world than the one he had left.

All of his friends, including his girlfriend were white, although students of color had reached out to him in friendship. He and his blonde girlfriend lived together several years before being married in her aunt's home. The ill-fated marriage ended in an annulment in less than a year, one of the many facts that I discovered later.

My fiancé had a troubled, Neo-Nazi, white male friend whom I chastised for his racially hateful language during our first and only meeting. After my interviews in Manhattan, we had joined him, his wife, and a friend of theirs for a live, nighttime concert in Central Park. My boyfriend pulled me aside before we left for Queens and said, "I've never heard anyone talk to him that way."

At my boyfriend's apartment, he forced himself on me without even asking me for my permission to touch me. We had no discussion of having consensual intercourse. It was excruciating painful, but when I told him so he kept forcing himself on me. Suddenly, he realized what he had done and that I had been a virgin. He said, "If I had known I would have waited until December."

In his mind, I was another woman to conquer, and he had planned to dump me if things did not go his way by a certain date. I was scared, believing that no one would want to marry anyone as old as me who was not a virgin. My boyfriend decided that we would get married after he saw that I was naïve and still wanted the relationship. I longed for a loving family and forgave my boyfriend since I knew he came from a broken home. He bought golden wedding bands from Macy's and really moved me with a golden, charm necklace of Cupid.

Some of my co-workers giggled when my boyfriend called me at the library, and I felt very much in love with him. I made my best effort to maintain balance in my professional and private life. For weeks, I traveled from Maryland to New York to find a full-time publishing position. I had always wanted a happy, healthy family, and my fiancé said he wanted me to be a part of his life in spite of my weaknesses. In fact, he *told* me he was going to marry me.

Before I left Maryland, I held another job at a stylish boutique owned by an Asian American woman in the Greenbelt Mall. My fiancé met her when he bought me a bold, color block red, black, and white summer dress. He could be generous at times, a quality I adored about him. My supervisor cried when I told her that I was leaving to be with my man in New York. I wore that dress to the lovely wedding of one of my fiancé's friends. We danced and enjoyed a delicious meal as the handsome groom and his blushing bride spent their first evening together as husband and wife. Suddenly, New York was not only a place where my career dreams could come true, but it was where my loneliness would end.

Old-fashioned and convinced of my fiancé's faithfulness, I purchased a white, satin wedding gown, pearl earrings, and white purse for my big day from my supervisor's store. A kind, European American classmate drove me to the bus station. I must have been the happiest passenger aboard the bus from Washington D.C. to New York City that day! When I arrived at the Port Authority that evening, I saw my man through the window. He looked anxious, as though he thought I would not arrive to meet him. His hands held the deepest red roses I had even seen. I nearly flew out of the bus to be by his side.

We rode the subway to Queens where he had leased an apartment, a third floor walk up. The next morning, we stocked up on groceries from the Asian supermarket down the street of our diverse Elmhurst neighborhood. My previous employer at Barnes and Noble Booksellers rehired me for part-time work while I interviewed elsewhere for full-time positions in my field. I met some of my fiancé's co-workers at the fashion company where he worked in IT. I admired him for his strong work ethic. He encouraged me while I was interviewing, sharing how he persisted until a good opportunity came along. Even though I could afford to buy them, my man insisted on buying my white bridal shoes. The salesperson thought we were just young kids getting ready for our senior prom!

Late one afternoon, an African American friend I had met during my first year in New York joined us for a meal at a Spanish restaurant in the West Village. She expressed her surprise that we were getting married since she had always been the one to talk to me about her relationship to her boyfriend. I asked her to be there for the wedding, and she agreed. It rained on my wedding day. I picked up my pastel rose bouquet from the Korean American florist, and we made our way to the subway. At City Hall, my friend who earned a degree in photography, tripled as my maid of honor and our witness. A European American woman justice of the peace officiated. Afterwards, we played around taking pictures at a church and gallery nearby. My friend caught the bouquet. For our luncheon, we enjoyed champagne and a savory meal with my friend at our favorite Indian restaurant in the West Village. We were married!

"Marriage is honorable among all, and the bed undefiled" (Hebrews 13:4). Intimacy at this level was new for me. I liked being a wife. The next week, I started balancing my roles as a wife, and a full-time staff member at a leading literary non-profit organization.

Going through the Fire and Exiting "the Habitation of Devils"

My husband grew up in a Catholic household, but had not really attended church for much of his life. I visited churches even when he slept in and invited him to come with me. Eventually, he did. I joined a church in Manhattan. One day, my husband told me that he wanted to relocate to Arizona. He had spoken with his mother about it. For most of the two years of our marriage, we had been in counseling. My doctor and my mentor suggested it. Our counselors said that New York can be hard on newlyweds. Wanting to make my husband happy, I agreed that we should move to be closer to his family. While my partner and I discussed children, I made the decision to focus on being myself, and not rushing the relationship as we had not been together for three years.

He was one of the few men in his family in several generations to have any formal education past the seventh grade with no babies to care for out of wedlock. My Asian American pastor instructed me to read the Book of Ruth in *The Holy Bible* which I did as I did not want to fight the man I had eloped with a few years prior.

What was I going to do in Arizona? I researched the universities there and applied to two of them to resume graduate studies in English. In the spring, I received an acceptance letter and teaching assistantship from one of the universities located in Phoenix, the state capitol.

I resigned from my job at a non-profit publisher and worked part-time at a stationery shop. We both seemed happy to be leaving the hustle and bustle of the big city. One evening, we attended our last jazz concert after a quiet, delicious dinner. We packed our belongings for shipping and flew to Phoenix. As I looked out of the airplane window at the red earth below, I thought about the American Indians who inhabited the region before the Europeans. The sky was clear, and I was hopeful about the future.

Our apartment was larger than our previous one with two bedrooms and two bathrooms. We swam in the pool and sat in the hot tub. The desert sun did not keep me from taking walks. With my husband's support, I began treatment with a naturopathic doctor whose husband was an expert in the field regionally. I lost all of the excess weight I had gained on one drug now known to cause diabetes. I felt healthy and strong.

For a few weeks, two faculty members provided teacher training. During my first year, I taught two classes of first-year English composition while taking courses for my program of study. On the first day of class, I asked them, "What does 'FUBU' stand for?" In loud unison, they proclaimed, "For us, by us!" While I owned more hip hop music than clothing, I did know the answer to the question before the students responded as a young woman of color myself. It was the enthusiasm with which they answered me that was so noteworthy. Hip hop is something that several of them identified with culturally across race.

Next, I asked the class why they often seemed not to care as an age group, and was told that they were going to die young, so they felt they might as well party. Once the ice was broken, I reviewed my expectations and requirements. I wrote in my diary often then.

September 2, 2000

I have been called. To ministry. To minister to young people. About them. They are the children. They are hurt. They are enraged. They are taking us out. Because we have not loved them like God commanded us to. That's why I teach. And smile.

Facilitating students learning about the importance of their voices and the power of the written word was my objective as a teacher. In the classroom community, everyone has something valuable to say, and language is the tool for communicating thought. My students worked individually during free write time where I encouraged them to let there thoughts flow onto the paper. They also discussed each others' progress by working collaboratively in writing workshops. I expected them to use their time out of class wisely before assignments were due as the syllabus, our contract, stated.

Typically, American freshmen do not understand the value of taking English. They want to write like actors talk in movies, and the way rapper rap and singers sing. My role as a college language instructor included preparing them to write papers in their chosen majors. Sunday *Holy Bible* lessons, daily chores, paid internships, part-time and full-time employment after college, and volunteering gave me space to honor the upright people who came before me. It also gave my students a real life example of how to earn a living with your education.

Some of the European American students in my class become hostile to reading literature written by people of color. Most of them had come from the suburbs in predominantly white cities. I explained patiently that knowing English well is a beginning as employers in places like the Southwest seek employees who are bilingual in Spanish, the first language of millions of people in this country. A student sought my opinion given his interest in creative writing. Only once did I put someone out of the class.

A few white students argued with me about their grades, but I was fair, showing them why I had given them such marks. My teaching philosophy was influenced by a late African American professor, a sociologist, who shared cool stories of the sixties and writing for television. He was not focused as much on grades as he was on studies understanding the culture from which African American literature was born. Most of my students completed my courses with passing grades.

I had no idea that Arizona State University, the institution that I hoped to earn my doctorate in English literature from, had haunted so many women of color, especially African American women, before me. There was a culture of retaliation and silence at ASU. My husband attended a dinner with me on campus the night that a Hispanic American scholar was the keynote speaker. I recall that most if not all of the other students at that particular conference event were European American. My spouse talked with me about the kind of environment that I would be in at ASU and remarked that some of them seemed quite ignorant.

Neither of us knew that we would be dealing with a tenured professor who operated like a sexual predator. One of the gaps on my transcript included African American literature from the 1960s and 1970s. This period is rarely taught in American English departments. Two of my classmates, one older, light-skinned black Latina woman and one international male student from Asia, encouraged me to take a course by a particular African American male professor, one of two in the entire department. I had never had nor seen a professor who stood like a goliath.

Nonetheless, as the new kid on the block excited about studying with my peers with scholars in the field of African American letters, I signed up for his course on black playwrights. I had read works by several of the writers independently, but some of the texts offered in the class were new to me. While my other two classmates remained friendly, one obese, African American woman seemed threatened by my presence. I learned later that she had an affair with this professor who was married to an immigrant white woman.

One of the highlights of studying theater during this time in my academic career was seeing *Joe Turner's Come and Gone* by August Wilson, one of the most brilliant playwrights in the history of American drama. I invited my husband to accompany me to the Phoenix restaurant where the class was meeting before going to a local theater to see the play. My handsome husband and I dressed up and joined the others just after they had ordered their food.

Unfortunately, the professor put his gargantuan, black hands on my shoulders and shook me like a rag doll during a group conversation about children and pets. Shock grabbed my stomach and was reflected on the faces of everyone around the table. Apparently, my classmates were intimidated by him, too, as no one said anything about his terribly ungodly behavior. I felt proud of my husband for not striking the professor because, after all, he had showed up for me. The professor had the nerve to try to taunt my husband while we were headed to the car to go to the theater. For our own comfort and safety, we sat several rows away from the rest of the group. We often went to the theater in New York, and we were determined not to allow an idiot intellectual to spoil our quality time together. However, the decisions I had to make after that night were life-changing and some of the most difficult choices I have ever had to make. At the end of the semester, I found out that I was one of the few students from the class who had earned an "A."

My young marriage was more fragile than it had been while my husband and I lived in New York for different reasons. We were working on our relationship by attending church, going to counseling, and sharing quality time together. Arizona posed new problems. Some of my spouse's family responded to our arrival and my being an addition to the family negatively. Additionally, I believe that several of his male relatives envied him his success, especially since his mother had brought him from Mexico to the United States at a young age. We had good careers in computer science and education, a nice apartment home, and a new car. More importantly, I believe we had love for each other as husband and wife. To this day, I pray for my ex-husband because I experienced such blessings in marriage and from forgiving him for the hurt.

By the grace of God, I had survived the first year in ASU's English doctoral program. When I withdrew from the institution in 2009, one of my dear friends from Asia, a young man studying linguistics, had died suddenly. What hurt ever so deeply was also the death of an African American female friend from Oberlin College. This woman made history in the music community and trained me on the radio station equipment. I even earned a FCC license. My Saturday morning show ran under the title, "Ladies of Jazz." Bessie Smith, Ella Fitzgerald, Sara Vaughn, Billie Holiday, Alberta Hunter, and composers Duke Ellington and Count Basie were the greats who could be heard on my program. I learned how to enjoy music more from my friend. She died single, unmarried, and childless at age 36.

I received a call one afternoon offering me a research position in African American literature with the professor my colleagues said we all needed to work with to earn our degrees. A few months had passed since his stupidity at the restaurant in Phoenix. The shock of it was not as strong as it had been. I needed graduate research experience on my curriculum vita as well as the extra income since my husband had become very controlling about money even for groceries.

A counselor suggested how to talk about my work with the professor. After accepting the position, I picked up the library card and materials from his office door. The book on Southern folklore did not surprise me. The writing about genitalia size, graphic hip hop lyrics, race and personal ads in newspapers caught me completely off guard, and I shared my concerns with my husband. Was this scholarly material? With all of the writing that could be done about African American writers, especially from contemporary times, why was a tenured professor of color dabbling in pop culture dribble?

I made edits, returned the material, and told the professor not to call my home. He crossed boundaries by emailing me that he had visited the church my husband and I attended but did not see us there. My husband sometimes felt threatened that I knew other African American men, but if I had wanted to marry a man just because he was African American, couldn't I have done so before I'd married him? I'm black. I shared with him my experiences at work because I loved him, and wanted him to believe in my dream of earning a Ph.D. and having a family near loved ones.

However, my husband became more suspicious and threatened. He talked of his first wife, a white woman, and how she had had an affair, left him, remarried, and had a baby. We tried counseling after I left him for a few days, but our reconciliation was not to be. I filed for divorce then informed my supervisors what course I would not be able to teach. I moved into a more affordable apartment and opened a mail box, cutting ties with the deceptive, African American church folk who tried to force me into a dangerous situation with my soon to be ex-husband.

My sister-friends from college sent me several hundred dollars which helped me with my expenses. My parents staged an act to force me back to my husband, but failed to gain control of my life. Knowing I was a brokenhearted, black, female, in a barrio apartment separated from mi amado me, my mother raced out to

Arizona but did not leave her hotel contact information. I had asked her not to come out as a few good friends had given me money to start over, and I had a workable schedule. I saw her at a local outlet mall and a classmate who was with me started towards her to be a third party, but Mama ran away, angry, and confused. My father made threatening phone calls and sent an ugly fax to the department office. How could this be happening? I sometimes cry because more than any degree, I have always wanted a happy, healthy family.

During that dramatic time in my life, the Lord God blessed me with a wonderful co-teaching position for an African American literature survey course with a kind, Christian, European American woman professor. A Southerner as well, she won me over when she offered me the co-teaching position. Together, we taught over sixty students about the African oral tradition, slave narratives, late nineteenth century writing, and the Harlem Renaissance. My multicultural students wanted to learn of the great contribution of African American writers to this country. This was an experience of great joy.

After that time, I worked in retail and at another college, perhaps overcompensating for all that had recently happened in my life. I fell into mourning and became anorexic. Lonely and in need of money, I permitted the woman from the black playwrights class to become my roommate. It was an ill-matched situation. One night, I went to the hospital with her because I had felt ill all day long. Unfortunately, they failed to admit me. My roommate abandoned me in the parking lot.

I arrived in a cab back at the apartment complex hours later, but never made it into my front door. I was raped repeatedly by a tall, lanky white man with a small, Hispanic roommate. I lost consciousness and may have been drugged. He cut my right elbow. I was found about 12 hours later, after I had passed out near the center of town. I spent weeks in the hospital in March, and again in May when I was readmitted for anxiety attacks. One nurse tech informed me of my victim's rights, and the evening news reported another attack while I was in the hospital. I went to the leasing office and started crying after I reported the crime, and the manager dropped me off at the police station.

Since no one came out to meet with me after nearly an hour, and nearly decided to come back another day. Just then two male, Tempe police officers led me into a room with a teddy bear on the sofa. I picked it up and answered their questions as best I could. They took me home in the police car and said whether or not I decided to press charges, they were going to do so. I thought about it all for a second and told them I wanted them to put him away. Sheriff Joe Arpaio's deputies posted a red and white sign on the apartment where the assault occurred. I was told by a nurse who visited my home that the suspect had been captured some time later. A neighbor confirmed that she had seen the authorities meeting with my landlord soon after the attack. The police arrested what turned out to be a serial rapist, and I flew to my mother's apartment home in Florida to convalesce.

In Florida, a compassionate, European American male doctor listened to me speak of the past year and prescribed medication. A women's center gave me a grant for counseling. The kind, European American woman who met with me drew a genogram showing how my grandmother, my mother, and I had all experienced abuse in our marriages. At that moment, I asked God to break the cycle of domestic violence in the feminine line of my family by preventing me from having children with a sick man. I vowed to be the one who would make the change and reverse this horrible generational curse.

The doctor and the counselor agreed that I should return to ASU and complete my studies for the Ph.D. I returned to the university and filed a discrimination complaint against the aggressive professor, who I learned later from a European American teacher had victimized other students. The Lord blessed me with an ally who had years of legal experience and a true heart for protecting the rights of young women scholars. A mixed woman lawyer with American Indian ancestry, she intervened to help me protect my education and income, citing the numerous times that she had interceded for other women graduate students.

At one point, I was shocked when she revealed how an affirmative action office personnel member had confiscated my U.S. mail addressed to her and faced severe penalties for doing so. At predominately white educational institutions of higher learning in America, qualified students from African American, Hispanic American, and American Indian ethnic backgrounds continue to face rampant intimidation. They face threats just for people of color where unjust laws and tradition formerly kept us locked out.

I applied to several on campus positions while at my mother's place and was made a few offers. I accepted a teaching position but was offered an advising assistantship a short time into training. Resigning from the teaching job, I praised God on the inside and agreed to serve African American and international students who utilized resources in Student Services under an African American male supervisor. When black students in my charge complained that the black faculty at ASU were often unavailable during office hours, I listened and took what action I could as a graduate assistant and master's degree level teacher.

One young African American woman student had also been harassed by the professor who harassed me when he, according to her account, talked about his failed relationships with African American women who he said all have "[bad] attitudes." I was proud of her for completing her bachelor's degree and entering graduate school, but felt concerned when she became a single mother with a boyfriend.

In another case, a student worker in the office I shared with several colleagues came to me for advice. Another top student went all the way to New York where he was published in an academic journal during his graduate school program of study in mathematics. I listened to God's whisper and prayed for him continually after I no longer saw him where I was working on-campus. When I had first heard the student play the classical guitar at the office Christmas celebration, I knew he was gifted. However, he was somewhat invisible because of his American Indian heritage. Continuously, I prayed for his safety and success since I did not see him at ASU anymore. One afternoon, I was tutoring a client at a local coffee shop when I saw him. I excused myself and found out that he had listened to my advice and gone to New York University for graduate school where he was studying for a master's degree. I thanked God for instructing me to pray for him as he was successful and well-suited to mentor his younger relatives who needed to know what a college education held in store for them. In public education in America, there are too many immoral, lazy people.

Late one afternoon, I walked in front of the student center where an enraged European American male in a suit nearly collided with an Indian male riding a bicycle. He cursed at him and then marched on. I asked my dark, Asian brother if he was okay and stood silently with him for a few minutes. Had such people learned nothing in the past fifty years?

I am reminded of Indian Prime Minister Indira Gandhi who stated, "My grandfather once told me that there are two kinds of people: those who work and those who take the credit. He told me to try to be in the first group; there was less competition there."[58] Over the course of two years in the Office of Student Life, I created a guest speaker series to introduce students to successful people of color in the community, collaborated with colleagues to invent an online career and scholarship website, and edited *MOSAIC*, an African Diasporan student magazine. I advised students, many of whom were first generation, on being successful undergraduate scholars regardless of barriers. On Sundays, I worshipped with other young adults sometimes on campus, and participated in a Campus Crusade for Christ and an interdenominational evangelistic outreach during final exam week.

October 27, 2001

We did it!

Little Princess Soldier had a successful first run tonight at the Prism (SLAB) Theatre. The small house was full (70 seats). Four people came out to support me. I was touched. None of the younger undergrads from the community came out. Maybe tomorrow night I'll go on the last night, Monday, and take them a small token of appreciation. T. and K. work extremely well together. I'm proud of them. My professor did a great job with them.

I am this close to quitting ASU. Tomorrow I'm going to the thrift store to look at work clothes. Unfortunately, I won't be able to dry clean anything before Monday when I plan on going to Super Recruiting Day to interview. Maybe I'll go to the mall instead. I can find something for $20 I'm sure. I want a part-time job, an extra 10-15 hours per week. I need to save money for a car. I want to leave AZ in the late spring or summer and go somewhere where people are more alive, were there's less stealth and more wealth, more of my people and more vibrant arts. The Ph.D. is not important to me, not as important as doing art and being myself. I want to step up my writing but feel I need to be around other serious Black writers. That's not going to happen here. I need to leave.

November 24, 2001

Talked to C. She exudes such confidence even though she's going through such drama with her ex-husband. She reminded me to just give credit to God for the good things He has done for me.

#1-A new apartment! I'm closer to school than I was before, walking or biking. I am out of that rough neighborhood. I'm still getting a feel for this one, but I do know that I sleep better at night, that there are no termites or bushes blocking my view on the walkway. And I have a dishwasher, a microwave, and a patio as part of the lease! I have as D. once wished for me moved up. Still need to unpack the office and connect my computer.... Need to make a budget list for the next two week's expenses so that I don't need to take out another loan.....Why do I need another job? To pay a lawyer to get the divorce trial over and done with and not pushed back again.

After 9/11, the Board of Trustees and ASU alumni elected an East Coast Columbia University Ivy League scientist to be the new President Dr. Michael Crow following Dr. Lattie Coor. Dr. Crow re-engineered the climate of the entire state university system with higher expectations and real money in addition to the athletics program. Ground was broken downtown Phoenix for a much overdue medical school, and the U of A and Tucson campuses began to cross-list courses with ASU instead of the three schools being rivals. I attended Dr. Crow's inauguration thanks to Asian American staff, and was invited as a student leader to meet privately with him and his secretary. I used that opportunity to ask him to clarify his vision on diversity in higher education and to voice concerns about being a woman of color graduate student. He graciously wrote an essay for *MOSAIC* and often met with students on the various campuses.

My greatest trial came when an Iraqi cab driver assaulted and stalked me in 2004. I had initially ridden in his taxicab to get to work in a department store in Scottsdale. A few times afterward, he drove me and my former roommate who had a form of arthritis around when we went shopping. At that time, I was prescribed and taking medication to help me to sleep. I did not know that the man would become obsessed with me and that they had discussed me when I was not around. Initially, I did not even know where he was from.

My neighborhood was not on the bus line and in the middle of it was a large pub. Sometimes homeless men would wander around, drinking alcohol. I just wanted a safe, affordable ride home. He would be drunk and said that my ex-roommate was "jealous." I felt like the Ethiopian Andromeda, the love of Perseus in Greek mythology, awaking each night to a waking nightmare with a fiend. During this time, Americans and NGO workers were being kidnapped and beheaded. I threw away my TV.

Thanks be to God, one quick thinking, European American male officer chased him away from my door very late at night after I had taken my medication and instructed me, "If he comes back again, do not open the door." With my comprehensive exams and an opportunity to teach a theater workshop coming up, I persisted in going to school and working on campus. However, terrified, my counselor, a European Jewish American male of approximately my same age, knew something was wrong. When women at ASU shuffled me around to different offices, he sent me to the hospital—at least once. The hospitals were not paying attention. I never received a rape kit.

One early morning around three a.m., the Holy Spirit commanded me to get up out of the futon that was my bed, pack a bag with my belongings, and leave the apartment. Immediately, I grabbed a designer bag and put into it my *Holy Bible*, a dress, and my wallet. My cell phone and U.S. passport were gone, so I walked to the public park where there were payphones to call for help. The phone I picked up was broken, so I walked the several miles to the hospital emergency room. A kind, young European American male doctor sat beside my bed until I was admitted to a hospital in Scottsdale. Although I eventually offered information about it, the doctors—one Asian American, one European American—failed to ascertain that I had been raped because they did not ask the right questions.

I cannot remember a female nurse being in the room when I was questioned by this pair who paid more attention in my chart, to the acne on my face than why I would be in an emergency room at three in the morning. An Asian American male doctor growled, "You can go on your black woman rape crusade if you want to. I am an Asian American male. I have it worse than you do." When another African American woman was admitted to the same unit of the hospital, we consoled each other by sharing stories about the taboo of being black and receiving counseling. Moreover, black women are resented for needing help after centuries of being stereotyped as super strong.

The effeminate but huge African American male case manager assigned to assist me was aggressive and indifferent. He made a crazed deal with a con artist, drug trade couple that were housed in the home for women in transition. They stole all of my worldly possessions save a backpack and the clothes I was wearing. that were housed in their home for women in transition. Bereft and in shock that thousands of dollars of artwork, books, clothing, shoes, music, and items of sentimental value like family and college photos were gone. I felt numb and less valuable than a dog in an animal shelter.

I stood up to the case manager until I found a space in a reputable women's shelter. I wished that I had been fortunate to be in such an environment as a child. At the women's shelter, I told several of the women that I was a writer and had been enrolled in school when I suffered the assaults. One by one, they opened up to me—black, white, Asian, American Indian, Christian, Muslim, Hispanic—about their circumstances and dreams for themselves and for their children. I felt honored and very loved by the God who plucked me out of harm's way and placed me beside my sisters and the innocents.

We attended workshops on breaking the cycle of domestic violence. We made collages. Groups of us took turns cooking large, delicious meals for everyone using our food stamps and public assistance money. We had the freedom to go off the grounds to take care of needed business during the day and to work at night if we needed to do so. The staff seemed to care deeply about women living lives free of brutality. The shelter's director is a father with daughters. I received a grant to find housing and the newfound courage to be the one to create change in my family.

After two months, I found a roommate in a house then moved to a safer situation in a condo with another young Christian woman. I did not attend ASU for about a year, but I received the best education of my life during that time. With my *Holy Bible* and a library book on Paul's letter to the Roman Christians, I realized the power of the questions the saint poses about the strength of our faith: "What shall separate us from the love of Christ? Shall tribulation, or distress, or persecution, or famine, or nakedness, or peril, or sword? As it is written: 'For your sake we are killed all day long; we are accounted as sheep for the slaughter'" (Romans 8: 35-36).

For about two years, I participated in a sexual assault recovery therapy group. The agency and women there who were also crime survivors were there when my family of origin was not. I read and re-read books by African American women rape survivors who had become activists healing and for social change.

A Christian counselor, an older European American woman with a background in the arts, told me how precious I am and advised that I was "being tested." She worked in the prisons and had seen the damage violent men could do to women. She asked me if I would be willing to help someone else who had also been raped. Would my wounds turn to hatred, self-destruction, or self-pity? My counselor encouraged me to date, saying, "You are waiting for your bridegroom."

Ironically, my first dating experience came while I sat in an Internet café. I responded harshly at first when the tall, dark-haired stranger offered to buy me a coffee, but my heart softened when he brought me back the biggest, sweetest, warmest cup of hot tea I have ever had. We went out for two nights during which time I found out that he was Turkish, had been divorced, and was on business in the US. He was affectionate even though I set firm physical boundaries and encouraged me in my writing career. I knew God had His Hand on me and that He expected me to "trust in [Him], and do good" (Psalm 37:3).

I pushed passed the grief of losing all of my books and went to the Goodwill and found the first book of my new life, *My Name is Asher Lev* (1972) by Chaim Potok, the story of a Jewish boy from Brooklyn who liked to paint.[59] With a lot of book knowledge but barely a clue about healthy relationships, I went to a Christian bookstore in Downtown Phoenix and invested in as many new and used books on love, dating and marriage, prayer, and women of faith that I could afford, maybe $30.

I shifted my focus from book titles on literary criticism to how much God wants my heart, and Jesus Christ's desire to give me "life" and "more abundantly" as in John 10:10. I poured over Reverend Charles Schuller's *Be Happy You are Loved* (1986)[60] and *Tough Times Never Last But Tough People Do*! (1984).[61] I became encouraged and strong on the inside as God healed me. I decided to enter a student book collecting contest. My collection was small, but I believed it to be valuable. After submitting an essay on my collection about books on love throughout the ages with a bibliography, I was interviewed by the judges. A friend and I attended the awards ceremony where I received a $100 dollar prize for my effort. Love had won.

A few European American women in academia have actually said to me openly that they blamed African American women for taking their scholarships. This is puzzling and got on my nerves since some white women benefit from affirmative action, too. This is racially hateful and ridiculous as the struggles of African American people and women are linked. I would often say to myself that, no matter what happened to me during my studies at ASU, no one could take away my bachelor's and master's degrees and the wisdom I had gained while earning them.

My suffering became a bundle of experiences that God used to empower me to reach out to students who faced unique challenges because of disabilities. I tutored students with varied abilities and found it to be important work. I saw the Lord do miracles in students' lives. In one instance, a spunky blind student had repeated a course but defied discrimination, re-enrolled, earned an "A," and graduated from ASU. Two other students, one Hispanic American male and one European American female, were accepted and enrolled in their top choice graduate schools in spite of their disabilities. In the time that I have worked in education, I have seen many students that were labeled "disabled" beat out mediocre students who felt entitled to good grades.

Praise God for the grandmother raising her grandchildren because her daughter, who was battling drug addiction, earned her bachelor's degree after I worked with her as a tutor! I saw the Lord Jesus Christ do miracles in students' lives. A parent whose son was beginning his studies at ASU thanked me for talking about my experience and success. Faculty members from a local high school and the university asked me to be a guest lecturer for their students.

In one class on Toni Morrison's novel, *The Bluest Eye* (1970),[62] none of the students knew that there had been a civil war in America from 1861 to 1865.[63] I went to the whiteboard in this teaching moment, wrote the dates of the war, and drew a map of the Transatlantic Slave Trade.[64] The professor of the course and I discussed the poor preparation students receive in school districts that omit crucial facts about US history. In another instance, I conducted a workshop with English-speaking bilingual high school students. They created colorful posters of their own poetry and learned about African American poetry. My Spanish language skills served as a bridge in a bilingual setting.

The year was 2008 and the community college which hired me had just experienced a shooting on-campus. Presidential politics captured international attention with the strong "Yes We Can" campaign of Senator of Illinois Barack Obama, an African American man. At the Phoenix school, the administration and authorities tried to figure out how and why the incident occurred. It is safe to say that we as faculty simply wanted to teach students in safety. I had my own lesson in dealing with this during that semester, one that showed me the community colleges in Maricopa County are perplexed and need support in protecting faculty and students.

Originally, the administrative assistant emailed me about the courses I would be teaching. The enrollment for the African American courses was too small, however, so the classes did not make. I agreed to teach composition courses for the fall. In addition to having two weekday morning groups, I would teach a Saturday morning pre-college success composition course. How blessed I felt to have been chosen to teach! When the manager at the apartment complex of my choice heard that I was a teacher, she told the leasing agent to give me a monthly discount on my rent. I had found favor with the right people according to God's perfect will, and it felt wonderful.

My weekday morning classes required me to wake up by 5:30 am. Without a car, I rode two buses into work a few days a week and on Saturday. I slept on an air mattress but wore quality, professional clothing to work. It was important for me to represent the best for my students so that they had a picture of success in their minds. In fact, one of their assignments required them to do an oral presentation on their future career or idea for a business. I introduced them to the career center on campus since they needed to prepare for a better future.

Additionally, some of my students were parents. The reports stunned me in their hope for the future and specificity of what it would take to reach the goals they had set. During our discussions, I questioned the wisdom of overspending on popular European and hip hop designer jeans and sportswear, and encouraged my students to invest in at least one interview appropriate outfit. I focused my grading on the verbal delivery of the report and on the writing. None of my students were born stupid. I assigned passages from Dr. Ben Carson's autobiography *Gifted Hands* (1990).[65] Carson, the renown neurosurgeon, was raised with his brother by an African American, functionally illiterate single mother who prayed and pushed him to excel—and he did. My students' positive response to such assignments proved that they wanted to earn college degrees and "be somebody."

It was in the Saturday class that I faced my greatest challenge in the person of one tall African American male student. He arrived a week after the class had started. He came in singing "50 Cents" hip hop lyrics about birthdays and sex. He had just turned eighteen years old. I spoke candidly to the small group about the positive sacrifice of choosing a college career in spite of the ridicule of those who said they "thought they were white." Giving my own experience of being called "white girl" by my peers who did not value education, I opened up the floor for my students' experiences. The eighteen-year-old confided that he was the only one in his neighborhood to make it to college. My other students were of Latino and Asian descent. My youngest student, L., was Black and Latino and seemed to look up to T.

Several of my students had work experience. It was not required for them to do the oral presentation, but it was necessary that they sit down and write out what career they wanted to work when the future arrived. I was concerned about T.'s being late to class and playing around in the halls with different young women. Moreover, I found his performance in class to be problematic. It took him abut five minutes to write one sentence on the blackboard. Maybe he thought basketball players do not need to know how to use English, but my job as the teacher was to show him the truth in preparation for the future. The rest of the class waited patiently as he finished his sentence, and no one ridiculed him because of his writing skill level.

What really made it difficult for me to teach at the community college began before the semester started.

I met with an European American teacher about her syllabus and found out her low expectations for students. Yes, it stung when she sat in the lunchroom with a group of other European American women faculty and, as a leader on the senate, mouthed how doctoral students should not be allowed to teach. However, a patriotic Christian Mexican American faculty member who could recite whole passages from documents by the Founding Fathers, and an African American woman faculty member welcomed and encouraged me.

I did not need to be anyone's favorite, but I did need intervention to direct students in the right way when issues came up. An advisor for the program and I met with T. She saw the concerns I had written up on him each week and decided to recommend that he see the school counselor. My colleague was Latina as was the dean of the program. Some time later, I spoke with the other program advisor, an African American male, who told me to have T. come and meet with him. The student resisted all counseling and did not go to either of the meetings. However, he was still allowed to participate in the program and to come to class.

It was just too much. Here he was saying he wanted to be like frontrunner Barack Obama who was at that time running to be U.S. President, but he rejected sound advice. He could barely write a sentence. When he started to disrupt my class, I had to draw the line. M., the Asian student who was older and had a degree elsewhere in addition to his own business, sat with him to share his homework. T. flipped out jealously. M.'s project was on becoming a pharmacist. T. insulted him by calling such a career "drug dealing." Next, he started chasing one of the Latina young women around the chairs in the circle.

I immediately told him to stop his behavior as we went up to settle the issue with the dean and advisors in a conference room. I reported T.'s behaviors and said I did not feel safe around him and wanted him out of my class. His mother arrived to fuss at me, but the decision was made. Where was she when her son needed someone to help him with his behavior and homework? What really troubled me was that it seemed like they had admitted a student to a program because he was a black male from an urban area. What about the eligibility requirements?

I knew there would be repercussions for taking a stand as a new adjunct faculty member, but I had to think about the safety of all of my students. I typed a letter and sent it to my supervisor in the Language Arts Department that same day. In the end, feeling undervalued and unsafe but grateful for the time I spent teaching students, I let the job go and moved on. I received a positive response from the administration after sending a letter to them about the issues I saw that needed to be addressed to make the campus safer, and a better college in the community.

How proud I felt at Commencement when students who had benefited from our services walked across the stage to receive their degrees, some with internships and jobs awaiting them! There is no greater reward than when students "get it," they learn the lesson you have taught them, and apply it to their studies and, hopefully, their lives.

When Barack Obama answered this African American woman in graduate school after I wrote to him, it was in the form of an appearance at the university where I studied and worked and in a letter. At the time, he was a senator from Illinois with a distinguished background in community activism, and a scholarship at Harvard University. As I write this memoir, he is the *first* African American President of the United States of America. When I was a girl, my father asked me quietly if I believed this country would always be run by white men. I was pensive and quiet then.

However, real grown up circumstances including being raped by an Iraqi cab driver and living below the poverty line pushed me to write to the man contending to lead from the White House. Obama appeared at Hayden Lawn at Arizona State University one sunny day in October, 2007 to a huge, peaceful crowd of about 7,000. I remember that sunny day because I had worn my Black History Month colors red, black, and green and later co-facilitated a workshop with a colleague on finding funding and surviving as a graduate student for Preparing Future Faculty.

An Arabic student stood next to me in the attentive crowd and expressed surprise at how nice I was to him. This was what we organized for change through Obama for: peace and harmony between diverse people within our American democracy. I voted for the first time earlier in college and thank God for the African American Civil Rights Movement leaders like Ella Baker[67] and Fannie Lou Hamer[68] who focused on educational access and human rights for disenfranchised women of color and their families.

As Indian human rights and Independence leader Mahatma Gandhi proclaimed, "Be the change you want to see in the world."[69] There were so many students in

Arizona and around the country who were involved in voter education during the last presidential race, and I felt proud to be a part of a historic campaign. When President Obama spoke at Commencement at ASU, my women mentees from Africa and the Caribbean graduated with undergraduate and graduate degrees. It was so rewarding to know that they were well-prepared for the future and to meet proud family members.

I completed and passed my oral and written exams in 2007, but my heart was no longer in my program of study because of the brutality I had experienced in the department and off campus. How could I hang a degree on my wall from university system that refused an honorary doctorate to the President of the United States, an African American man who later won the Nobel Peace Prize? Unfortunately, my dissertation chair's mother died. One of my younger brothers and his family came to visit me which was both consoling and fun. I am an aunt now. Gathering my courage, I met with the concerned dean in the graduate college with a kind African American woman friend to discuss options for completing my degree program. In December, 2009, I withdrew from ASU. I grieved, extremely disappointed, but knew that I will always be a child of God: "Beloved, let us love one another, for love is of God; and everyone who loves is born of God and knows God" (I John 4:7).

My identity as a Christian empowered me to serve others and to survive unbelievable odds at a public university in the Southwest. As a rape survivor, I made presentations at churches about the biblical responsibility that American churches have to minister to victims, and to change a misogynist society that does not yet understand the meaning and practice of treating women and girls as God's sacred creations.

For several months, I operated Brown Sugar Productions, a business that provided résumés, tutoring services, and gifts. While working at a Mediterranean restaurant, I sold sweet potato pies in the community. They were very popular. A kind, European American female minister at church, who served women and children for years, counseled me about my future. We discussed dating, family, and teaching, her former career. I became more optimistic and, with the help of a good Jewish male friend, left the Arizona desert, returning to my hometown in Florida. As I celebrated the Thanksgiving and Christmas holidays with family and friends whom I had not seen in years, I wondered, as the first woman teacher in my line, where I belonged and where my life was headed: "Strength and honor are her clothing; and she shall rejoice in time to come" (Proverbs 31:25).

I joined a local church by invitation and began to reflect on my experiences of the past decade.

What is it Like Being Dad's Daughter?

hat is it like being Dad's daughter, his little girl then and his adult daughter now? Writing about him now as a retired college humanities teacher who is not yet fifty, I am grateful for having any good memories of my biological father.

What was it like being Dad's daughter in high school? It was that once-in-a-lifetime audition at the city's first fine arts magnet school several days after the nine-week quarter had already begun. Now a legendary, local artist called "the best artist in Jacksonville" by some, my father taught me how to draw and to paint. When I was about five years old, he gave me a bright pink pencil case that folded over and closed with a magnetic strip on the side. One of my brothers was old enough to hold a pencil and received a light blue one. I remember finding it on the wooden kitchen table, glowing like a rosebud. How I loved to watch my Dad's strong, dark brown hand curve around pencils and paintbrushes! His handwriting flourished at the end of each of his acrylic and oil paintings.

As a small child, I liked how Dad believed in bold color. Many in the ultraconservative congregation my parents were married in shunned any hue that was not a dull blue, green, grey, taupe, or highly dignified. Not my Dad. My Dad had a Polaroid photograph of himself with the caption, "I'm a bad Dad." The discrimination and hostility he faced after coming back from the war in Vietnam forced him to find his own opportunities, and to make his own way. He opened his business as an architectural draftsman and a commercial artist in the garage. In the Nazarene church on the corner, he painted a mural of the Lord Jesus being baptized by John the Baptist.

Dad believed in whipping children as a form of discipline. I remember being beaten twice in one night, the second time for not liking the first licks. It did not kill me. I grew up with two brothers who needed discipline a few times. I know I will not allow my husband to hit my girl children. It could make her expect to be abused by men. My father sensed that I was tough and did not hit me after that. I was like a female soldier. Even though I loved him, I prayed that we would leave Dad's house forever. *I hated his putting his hands on my beautiful, brown mother.* Females are not meant to be beaten.

Artistic talent flows in my veins, and my Dad encouraged me to draw and to paint by buying me markers, paint, and posters when he went to the art supply store. Accustomed to the smell of wet paint and cleaning fluid Dad used on his canvases as a commercial artist and architectural draftsman, I walked onto the campus of Douglas Anderson School of the Arts with energy and a wish to make it like Irene Cara and the other city kids on *Fame*.[70] The school was "established as an arts school in 1985."[71] Like Stanton, Douglas Anderson School of the Arts began to educate "African American students" in "1922."[72] The founder, Douglas Anderson, graduated from the "Tuskegee Institute," "completing his education in the carpentry division."[73] He and "W.R. Thorpe" led project.[74] "Nine years" after Anderson's death, "in 1945 The South Jacksonville School was named Douglas Anderson School."[75] For my audition, I drew a still life after being introduced to the examiner and shown to my space in one, sturdy chair. Within a short time, I celebrated with Dad having been given a coveted spot in the eleventh grade visual arts program.

The Advanced Placement American history teacher in my senior year was a young, European American woman. The small class had an enrollment of less than ten, and I was the only student of color. During a lesson on the Vietnam War, I began to think of my Dad's lecture to my brothers on the fact that the loss of human life is not funny and how hellish war conditions were.[76] In the films that we saw at school, young soldiers fired upon the enemy and were wounded. On clip showed a group of servicemen dancing and drinking at a nightclub where young Asian women were dancing.

Knowing that my father was sensitive about his time in the war, but wondering about his experience, I asked him to visit my class and talk to us. A white-haired, European American male substitute teacher sat at my teacher's desk on the day of my Dad's presentation. He brought in his US Army uniform and a framed picture of himself in his beret. We gasped when my Dad told us his weight and showed us his picture. My father spoke about the value of patriotism and showed slides of Asian schoolchildren. His voice became soft when he shared with us his friendship with a young, European American male standing on the beach smiling. I felt very proud of my father that day.

Later in my senior year, a substitute teacher asked me to help a South Korean visitor's daughter with her art lesson, and I did gladly. We became friends. I discussed prom with my mother and saw the prettiest red dress. I also spoke to a fellow about escorting me and hoped he had a friend. However, that plan fell through and I was disappointed. My father took me in my turquoise and black ensemble and my friend in her beautiful native dress to dinner and then he spent time with us at the prom. When I remember his thoughtfulness that evening, I am happy that he was there for me and am thankful.

My father is an elderly, disabled military veteran who spent most of his life giving back to society as an artist and a teacher. Parents get old, but children always have the biblical responsibility of honoring them. On a brief visit to Florida, I left a care package with information about health resources for my Dad. He relocated to an area with better services for military veterans and began to paint again. Before I left Arizona, I mailed my master's degree to him. When we spent part of the Thanksgiving holiday season today, he told me with tears in his eyes, "I am so proud of you."

As a girl, I longed for my father's affection and protection. Sharing his library about Christianity and world civilizations was his way of showing love to me. As an imperfect human being, he was able to give what he could. As a believer and an adult woman, I realize with thanksgiving how my Heavenly Father created my father and my mother and will always be there for me as Abba Father: "Yes, I have loved you with an everlasting love" (Jeremiah 31:3).

Abba, I love you back!

The Original, Soft Gentleness of African American Wise Women

*G*entle black women in America are complex, capable of softness and strength. Along with my sisters who hate being seen as black superwomen who emasculate African American men, I agree African American women need cross-cultural acknowledgement of our soft side.[77] We embody Mother Eve's original femininity as described in Genesis 1:27 and 2 of the *Holy Bible*: "So God created man in His Own image; in the image of God He created Him; male and female He created them."

Black women look like Creator God, not monkeys. Neither are we Mammies nor tragic.

"Attitude" is not a bad word. My seventh grade geography teacher, a stout, sweet African American woman who taught at Stanton during the era of segregation, showed me that "attitude determines altitude" by imparting instruction and wisdom to me each lesson even though the world may be ignorant and violent. My strength as a "mixed race" black sister must never be used to disrespect the women in my ancestral line nor the men whose bloody sweat and kindness created so much of the wealth of this nation and even Europe in the 1700s and 1800s. I am in this time empowered by my ancestors to build success from their sacrifice and shattered dreams. There is a generation alive now that needs the truth about the historic African American struggle that must be taught in our homes and in the schools. All of us who are human beings have red blood.

Yes, I have Indian in me!

On Being Beautiful, Black, and Brilliant

*B*eing beautiful, black, and brilliant is a blessing from God. During the end of my season as an educator out in the Wild, Wild West, an accomplished colleague encouraged me with the words, "Be medium." It was good advice and helped me to take a leap of faith. I recovered the joy of being myself at the kind words of a friend.

Sadly, American academia often seems to reward the extreme. For example, in the field of English literature, there is small percentage of pop professors famous for their disregard of students, and for writing trendy essays on Hollywood and homosexuality. Their classroom lectures lack real substance on British Empire, American literary traditions, and linguistics. Instead, these darlings of relativism, truly predatory creatures, cry out to an unknown deity about how they were rejected by ex-lovers and have been banished to roam from campus to campus because no one can afford to perpetually pay them superstar salaries.

Tragically, several of my classmates were abused by pseudo-teachers who bullied them outside of the classroom in extracurricular groups for being African American, Christian, virgins, and young.

Self-proclaimed "children of the sixties," these folk craved worship more than education, and caused havoc in their departments by their selfishness. I have heard of black women university professors who had sex with vulnerable, young women students who later suffered mental breakdowns or committed suicide after the affairs were exposed.

One New York-based English teacher advised me to never speak publicly in opposition to certain publishing giants due to their large, cult-like following, and personal viciousness. While working in the industry, I learned how truly non-literary it can be. Generally, my colleagues at non-profit organizations tended to more productive in promoting good literature and were more well-rounded. I turned down an ambiguous offer at a monthly women's magazine for a clear cut position deciding that philanthropy served a greater purpose than chasing celebrities. Choosing to follow my heart as a member of Generation X means rejecting materialism by focusing on building community. Today, there is too much emphasis on bling. My generation's greatest challenge may be to humbly pay homage to our ancestors, and the American heroes and she-roes of yesteryear by living with integrity in gratitude for their paving the way.

Despite the attempts of postmodernists and a small group of narcissistic, racially divisive black academics to downplay the role that race played in shaping African American literature and American society, the truth is that for decades African Americans were denied citizenship and membership in certain professional academic associations. Brown paper bag tests, illegal hiring and firing tactics after affirmative action policies were mandated, and other petty but harsh practices existed amongst faculty groups within predominantly white educational institutions in particular.

One would be wise to note how most of the black men at such places are married to non-black women. In fact, one white Jewish professor asked me why light-skinned African Americans often tend to be the first to be selected for posts in mainstream organizations. His question signaled frustration with the institutional-ized racism present in contemporary times within top colleges and universities, a system that now seeks to dismantle the HBCUs like Spelman College, often cre-ated by churches that ushered in a new era of American higher education after the Civil War.

Yes, brown-skinned women scholars and teachers fight for our lives within the Ivory Tower until God elevates us to new heights. Our insight in the middle of the racial spectrum can destroy us or empower us to lead others. The lingering reality of antebellum white male slave masters who sent their mixed race, African children secretly to be educated in what are now known as premiere liberal arts colleges means that African American and other faculty have a duty to teach their students the truth.

No matter how much misguided intellectuals try to distract from the American past by submerging their stubborn minds in the histories of, it is imperative that the truth be told. For example, imperial Asia and Latin America, the world's 17th-18th century ruling class made money off of the blood, sweat, and tears of African people. Thomas Jefferson, the third American President and author of *The Declaration of Independence,* fathered children with the enslaved African Sally Hemings, his wife's half-sister. Dire consequences would result from the centuries long exploitation of the African family victimized during slave trade.[78]

This novel moment of change has seen the children who benefited from a more integrated West produce a faith-based, global human rights movement as leaders in our local and national communities. Tutored in computers, diverse languages, and highly mobile, we resist easy categorization by following a path that streams from God's Heart. Our Heavenly Father is the One able to make the dream of restored humanity come true. "There is one body and one Spirit...one Lord, one faith, one baptism; one God and Father of all, who is above all" (Ephesians 4:4-6).

Being a young Christian African American woman educator has been the biggest blessing of my life. Teaching is extremely serious business because, as my Ethiopian brother, a renown paleontologist told me warmly after he made a presentation to my students, "You are changing people's lives." The violence I suffered may seem to be unbelievable to some, but my scars have become "beauty for ashes" as in Isaiah 61:3. My testimony as an overcomer is evidence that I am a real woman, truly loved, and used by the Creator and Jesus Christ the King.

Works Cited

"About AUCC." Web. 4 September 2012, <http://www.aucenter.edu>.

"About the Center." Web. 19 September 2012. <http://www.nypl.org>.

"About DA." Web. 25 September 2012. <www.da-arts.org>.

"About Dr. King." Web. 2 October 2012. <http://www.theking-center.org>.

"About the Library." Web. 5 October 2012, <http://www.auctr.edu>.

"About Us." Web. 20 September 2012. <http://www.talawa.com/productions.php.>

Ali, Maulana Muhammad, trans., *The Holy Quaran*. Dublin, OH: Islam Lahore, Inc., 2002.

Angelou, Maya. *I Know Why the Caged Bird Sings*. New York: Random House, 1970.

Appiah, Kwame Anthony and Henry Louis gates, Jr. *Africana: The Encyclopedia of the African and African American Experience. The Concise Desk Reference*. Philadelphia: Running P, 2003. 84-85, 908.

"Background." Web. 05 October 2012. <http://new.historic-ebenzer.org>.

"Biography: Benjamin E. Mays." Web. 2 October 2012. <http://www.morehouse.edu>.

"Black Power." *Africana: The Encyclopedia of the African and African American Experience. The Concise Desk Reference.* Appiah, Kwame Anthony and Henry Gates, Jr., eds. Philadelphia: Running P, 2003.

Busby, Margaret, ed. *Daughters of Africa: An International Anthology of Words and*

Writings by Women of African Descent and from the Ancient Egyptian to the Present. New York: Knopf Doubleday, 1992.

Carson, Ben and Cecil Murphey. *Gifted Hands: The Ben Carson Story.* Grand Rapids: Zondervan, 1990.

Cole, Johnnetta B. *Conversations: Straight Talk with America's Sister President.* New York: Anchor, 1994.

Cooper, Anna Julia. *A Voice from the South.* 1992. Edited by Mary Helen Washington. New York: Oxford U P, 1990.

Danquah, Meri Nana-Ama. *Willow Weep for Me: A Black Women's Journey Through*

Depression. New York: One World/Ballantine, 1999.

Dobson, James. *Preparing for Adolescence: How to Survive the Coming Years of Change.* Ventura: Gospel Light, 1978.

Douglass, Frederick. *Narrative in the Life of Frederick Douglass.* 1845. Preface by William Lloyd Garrison. Mineola, NY: Dover Publications, 1995.

Ellison, Ralph. *Invisible Man.* New York: Random House, 1952.

"Endesha Ida Mae Holland." Web. 20 September 2012. <http:// voices.cla.umn.edu/artistpages>.

Eyes on the Prize: America's Civil Rights Movement 1954-1985. American Experience. Based on the book written by Juan Williams. Introduction by Julian Bond. Prod. Blackside. PBS, 1988.

Fame. Dir. Alan Parker. United Artists. 1980.

"Fannie Lou Hamer: Woman of Courage." Web. 2 October 2012. <http://www.howard.edu/library>.

"Hans Christian Andersen: Fairy Tales and Stories." Web. 1 October 2012. <http://www.hca.gilead.org.il/>.

Hansberry, Lorraine. *A Raisin in the Sun*. 1958. Introduction by Robert Nemiroff. New York: Random House, 1988.

Hemenway, Robert E. *Zora Neale Hurston: A Literary Biography*. Foreword by Alice Walker. Champaign: University of Illinois P, 1980.

"History." Web. 2 October 2012. <www.ebony.com>.

"History in Brief." Web. 14 September 2012. <http://www.spelman.edu.>

Holland, Endesha Mae. *From the Mississippi Delta: A Memoir*. New York: Simon & Schuster, 1997.

Biography. Foreword by Alice Walker. Champaign: University of Illinois P, 1980

Hughes, Langston. "The Negro Mother." Web. 4 September 2012.   <http://www.famouspoetsandpoems.com/poets/langston_hughes/poems>.

Hurston Zora Neale. *Their Eyes Were Watching God*. 1937. Foreword by Mary Helen Washington. Afterword by Henry Louis Gates, Jr. York: Perennial, 1990.

"Indira Gandhi Quotes." Web. 29 September 2012. <http://thinkexist.com>.

Jahn, Janheinz. *Muntu: African Culture and the Western World*. Translated by Marjorie Grene. Introduction by Calvin C. Hernton. 1961. New York: Grove P, 1990.

Jakes, T.D. *Daddy Loves His Girls*. Lake Mary: Charisma House, 1996.

Jamison, Kay Redfield. *An Unquiet Mind: A Memoir of Moods and Madness*. New preface by the author. New York: Vintage, 1996.

Jones, LeRoi. *Dutchman and The Slave: Two Plays*. 1964. New York: Quill, 1971.

Kennedy, Adrienne. *Ohio State Murders*. New York: Samuel French, 1992.

King, Naomi. *O.P.P.* London: The X Press, 1993.

Knowles, John. *A Separate Peace*. New York: Scribner, 1959.

Lee, Harper. *To Kill a Mockingbird*. Philadelphia: J.B. Lippincott & Co., 1960.

"Linton Kwesi Johnson." Web. 29 September 2012. <http://www.lintonkwesijohnson.com>.

"Little Known HBCU Facts." Web. 3 October 2012. <http:thinkhbcu.org>.

"Mahatma Gandhi Quotes." Web. 29 September 2012. <http://thinkexist.com>.

Malcolm X. Dir. Spike Lee. 40 Acres & A Mule. 1992.

"Naomi Campbell." Web. 5 October 2012. <http://biography.com>.

The Net. Dir. Irwin Winkler. Columbia Pictures. 1995.

Oberlin College Theater Program Handbook, September 19, 2010. Web. 29 September 2012. <http://oberlin.edu>.

Pierce, Baker, Charlotte. *Surviving the Silence: Black Women's Stories of Rape*. New York: W.W.Norton, 2000.

Potok, Chaim. *My Name is Asher Lev*. New York: Knopf Doubleday, 1972.

Robinson, Lori S. *I Will Survive: The African American Guide to Healing from Sexual Assault and Abuse*. Foreword by Julia A. Boyd. New York: Seal P, 2002.

Rosewood. Dir. John Singleton. Warner Brothers, 1997.

Said, Edward. *Orientalism*. New York: Random House,1979.

Schuller, Robert H. *Be Happy You Are Loved*. Nashville: Thomas Nelson, 1986.

—. *Tough Times Never Last But Tough People Do!* New York: Bantam, 1984.

Shelley, Mary. *Frankenstein or The Modern Prometheus.* 1818. New York: Simon & Brown, 2012.

"Spelman College Founders." *The New Georgia Encyclopedia.* Web. 14 September 2012. <http://www.georgiaencyclopedia.org>.

"Stanton History." Web. 26 August 2012. <http://stanton. duvalschools.org>.

"The Souls of Black Folk." Web. 25 September 2012. <http:// www.bartleby.com>.

"The Two Gentleman of Verona." Davidson College RSC Learning. Web. 28 September 2012. <http://www3.davidson.edu.>

"Thomas Jefferson." Web. 29 September 2012. <http://www. monticello.org>.

"T.S. Eliot." Web. 5 October 2012. <http://www.poets.org>.

"Vietnam War." Web. 5 October 2012. <http://history.com>.

Wallace, Michele. *Black Macho and the Myth of the Superwoman.* New York: Dial P, 1979.

Wells, H.G. *The Invisible Man.* 1897. New York: Dover Publications, 1992.

"W.H. Auden." Web. 5 October 2012. <http://www.poets.org>.

"Who Was Ella Baker?" Web. 2 October 2012. <http://www. ellabakercenter.org>.

Wilson, August. *Joe Turner's Come and Gone.* New York: Plume, 1988.

Wright, Richard. *Native Son.* 1950. New York: HarperCollins, 1989.

About the Author

Veronica Y. Njeri-Imani attended Spelman College in Atlanta, Georgia and is a graduate of Oberlin College in Oberlin, Ohio. She holds a master's degree in English Language and Literature from the University of Maryland, College Park, and has taught various subjects at the university level. Her writing has appeared online, and she has appeared on national television for National Black Poetry Day. A community activist for the empowerment of women and girls, Njeri-Imani was born in Jacksonville, Florida and has traveled around the world.

Endnotes

[1]"The Souls of Black Folk." 25 September 2012. <http://www. bartleby.com.>

[2]"Harriet Tubman," *American Civil War.* 02 October 2012 <http:// www.americancivilwar.com/women/harriet_tubman.html>.

[3]"Hans Christian Andersen: Fairy Tales and Stories." 02 October 2012. <http://www.hca.gilead.org.il/>.

[4]"Stanton History." 26 August 2012. <http://stanton.duvalschools. org>.

[5]"Eyes on the Prize: America's Civil Rights Movement 1954-1985." Blackside. 1988. PBS.

[6]John Knowles, *A Separate Peace.* (New York Scribner, 1959).

[7]James Dobson, *Preparing for Adolescence: How to Survive the Coming Years of Change.* (Ventura: Gospel Light, 1978).

[8]Richard Wright, *Native Son.* 1950. (New York: HarperCollins, 1989).

[9]Zora Neale Hurston, *Their Eyes Were Watching God.* 1937. (New York: Perennial, 1990).

[10]Robert E. Hemenway, *Zora Neale Hurston: A Literary Biography.* (Champaign: University of Illinois P, 1980.

[11]Maya Angelou, *I Know Why the Caged Bird Sings.* (New York: Random House, 1970).

[12]Lorraine Hansberry, *A Raisin in the Sun.* (New York: Random House, 1958).

[13]Harper Lee, *To Kill a Mockingbird*. (Philadelphia: J.B. Lippincott & Co., 1960).

[14]Ralph Ellison, *Invisible Man*. (New York: Random House, 1952).

[15]H.G.Wells, *The Invisible Man*. (Mineola, NY: Dover Publications, 1992).

[16]Ellison.

[17]Tom Eyen, *Dreamgirls*. (New York: Geffen Records, 1981).

[18]"The Negro Mother," *Famous Poets and Poems*, 4 September 2012 <http://www.famouspoetsandpoems/poets/langston_hughes/poems>.

[19]"History in Brief," *Spelman College*, 14 September 2012, <http//www.spelman.edu>.

[20]"Spelman College Founders," *New Georgia Encyclopedia*, 14 September 2012, <http://www.georgiaencyclopedia.org>.

[21]See the Spelman College website for a timeline about the school's establishment, growth, and early administration.

[22]*Spelman College.*

[23]"About Dr. King," *The King Center*, 2 October 2012, <http://www.thekingcenter.org>.

[24]"Biography: Benjamin E. Mays," *Morehouse College*, 2 October 2012, <http://www.morehouse.edu>.

[25]"Background," *Ebenezer Baptist Church*, 05 October 2012, <http://new.historicebenzer.org>.

[26]"About AUCC," *Atlanta University Center Consortium, Inc.*, 4 September 2012, <http://www.aucenter.edu>.

[27]"About the Library," *Robert W. Woodruff Library at the AUC*, 5 October 2012, <http://www.auctr.edu>.

[28]Johnnetta B. Cole, *Conversations: Straight Talk with America's Sister President*, (New York: Anchor Books, 1994).

[29]Anna Julia Cooper, *A Voice from the South*, Mary Helen Washington, ed. (New York: Oxford U P, 1990).

³⁰Edward Said, *Orientalism*. (New York: Random House, 1979).

³¹Mary Shelley, *Frankenstein or the Modern Prometheus*. 1818. (New York: Simon & Schuster ,2012).

³²"Frankenstein." Dir. James Whale. Universal Pictures. 1931

³³Matthew Wright, ed., "Oberlin College Theater Handbook, September 19, 2010," *Oberlin College*, 29 September 2012, <http:oberlin.edu>.

³⁴Adrienne Kennedy, *The Ohio State Murders*. (New York: Samuel French, 1992).

³⁵"W.H. Auden," *Poets.org*, 5 October 2012, <http://www.poets.org>.

³⁶"T.S. Eliot," *Poets. org*, 5 October 2012, <http://www.poets.org>.

³⁷"Naomi Campbell," *Biography*, 5 October 2012, http://www.biography.com.

³⁸"Malcolm X." Dir. Spike Lee. 40 Acres & A Mule. 1992.

³⁹Margaret Busby, ed., *Daughters of Africa: An International Anthology of Words and Writings by Women of African Descent and from the Ancient Egyptian to the Present*. (New York: Knopf Doubleday, 1992).

⁴⁰"Linton Kwesi Johnson," *Linton Kwesi Johnson*," 29 September 2012, <http://www.lintonkwesijohnson.com>.

⁴¹"About Us," *Talawa Theatre Company*, 20 September 2012, <http://www.talawa.com/productions.php>.

⁴²"Endesha Ida Mae Holland," *University of Minnesota*," 20 September 2012, <http://voices.cla.umn.edu/artistpages>.

⁴³*University of Minnesota*.

⁴⁴"The Two Gentlemen of Verona' Study Guide for Teachers,"' *Davidson College RSC Learning*, 28 September 2012, <http://www3.davidson.edu>.

⁴⁵ *Davidson College RSC Learning*.

⁴⁶ *Davidson College RSC Learning*.

47Maulana Muhammad Ali, trans., *The Holy Quaran*. (Dublin, OH: Islam Lahore, Inc., 2002).

48"About the Center: Schomburg Center for Research in Black Culture," *New York Public Library*, 19 September 2012, <http://www.nypl.org>.

49"The Net." Dir. Irwin Winkler. Columbia Pictures. 1995.

50Janheinz Jahn, *Muntu: African Culture and the Western World*. (New York: Grove P, 1990).

51Frederick Douglass, *Narrative of the Life of Frederick Douglass*. 1845. (Mineola, NY: Dover Publications, 1995).

52"Rosewood." Dir. John Singleton. Warner Brothers. 1997.

53Kwame Anthony Appiah and Henry Louis gates, Jr., eds., "Black Power," *Africana: The Encyclopedia of the African and African American Experience. The Concise Desk Reference*. (Philadelphia: Running P, 2003), 84-85.

54Henry Louis Gates, Jr., *The Signifying Monkey: A Theory of African American Literary Criticism*. (New York: Oxford U P, 1988).

55LeRoi Jones, *Dutchman and The Slave: Two Plays*. (New York: Quill, 1971).

56"Little Known HBCU Facts," *Think HBCU*, 3 October 2012, <http://thinkhbcu.org>.

57"Indira Gandhi," *Think Exist*, 29 September 2012, <http://thinkexist.com>.

58Potok Chaim, *My Name is Asher Lev*. (New York: Knopf Doubleday, 1972).

59Robert H. Schuller, *Be Happy You Are Loved*. (Nashville: Thomas Nelson, 1986).

60Schuller, *Tough times Never Last But Tough People Do!* (New York: Bantam, 1984).

61Toni Morrison, *The Bluest Eye*. 1970. (New York: Knopf Doubleday, 2007).

62"Harriet Tubman," *American Civil War*, 1 October 2012, <http://www.americancivilwar.com/women/harriet_tubman.html>.

[63]"Transatlantic Slave Trade," *Africana*, 908.

[64]Ben Carson and Cecil Murphey, *Gifted Hands: The Ben Carson Story*. (Grand Rapids: Zondervan, 1990).

[65]"Who Was Ella Baker?," *Ella Baker Center*, 2 October 2012, <http://ellabakercenter.org>.

[66]"Fannie Lou Hamer: Woman of Courage," *Howard University*, 2 October 2012, <http://www.howard.edu/library>.

[67]"Mahatma Gandhi," *Think Exist*, 29 September 2012, <http// thinkexist.com>.

[68]"Fame." Dir. Alan Parker. United Artists. 1980.

[69]"About DA," *Douglas Anderson School of the Arts*, 25 September 2012, <http://www.da-arts.org>.

[70]"Vietnam War," *History*, 5 October 2012 2012, <http://history. com>.

[71]Michele Wallace, *Black Macho and the Myth of the Superwoman*. (New York: Dial P, 1979).

[72]"Thomas Jefferson," *Monticello*, 29 September 2012, <http:// www.monticello.org>.

CPSIA information can be obtained at www.ICGtesting.com
Printed in the USA
LVOW08s1811170715

446653LV00001B/22/P